Just getting started with FrameMaker?

Get free FrameMaker training

I've put together a quick course at techcomm.tools/free-fm-training to show you two things:

- Creating documents with FrameMaker will save you and your company money when you work efficiently
- You can easily learn the skills to edit content with unstructured FrameMaker in just a couple of hours

HTML5 Publishing training

I love finding out about who's reading my book, and the easiest way for me to get to know you is to bribe you with goodies!

When you visit techcomm.tools/html5 and tell me who you are, you'll get 3 free lessons on HTML5 publishing with FrameMaker. The lessons are part of my larger Digital Publishing with FrameMaker course, but the lessons are more than just an intro into the topic. They give you what you need to produce default output and improve the branding of your digital project.

GET FREE HTML5 PUBLISHING TRAINING

Scan this code or visit **bit.ly/html5-train** and I'll send you a 3-part video training series showing you how easy it is to get great online and mobile output from FrameMaker!

Need something else?

Tech Comm Tools offers online courses, live classes, and help with specific problems too.

Visit techcommtools.com or see the final page of the book for details.

i

About the Author

Matt Sullivan

Matt is the founder of Tech Comm Tools. Along with FrameMaker training and consulting available at www.techcommtools.com, Matt helps organizations improve their use of video and interactive media within their documentation, and delivering that content to online and mobile users.

Matt is an Adobe Tech Comm Partner, Adobe Certified Trainer, Adobe Certified Expert, and an Adobe Community Professional. He has produced new feature videos for the past 4 versions of FrameMaker and the Adobe Technical Communication Suite.

He is also the author of

- FrameMaker - Structured Authoring Workbook (2019 Release)
- FrameMaker - Structured Authoring Workbook (2017 Release)
- FrameMaker - Structured EDD Development Workbook (2017 Release)
- FrameMaker - Working with Content (2017 Release)
- FrameMaker - Creating and Editing Content (2015 Release)
- Publishing Fundamentals: Unstructured FrameMaker (version 11)

You can find information about print and eBooks of these titles at www.techcommtools.com/books/

Both structured and standard (unstructured) courses are available at www.techcomm.tools/training-courses

Stay up-to-date with #techcomm content by signing up for his free newsletter at www.techcommtools.com/email-list/

Please connect with Matt (*mattrsullivan* on social platforms) and visit the Tech Comm Tools Facebook page at www.facebook.com/tc2ls/

When not working with clients, (and outside of AYSO seasons) you'll find Matt surfing with Marianne and his two daughters, or enjoying other beach or snow activities.

Reach Matt directly by emailing him at matt@techcommtools.com

FRAMEMAKER 2019 STRUCTURED EDD DEVELOPMENT

A workbook for self-paced or instructor-led training

Matt R. Sullivan

Important Notice

Contents

Chapter 4: GeneralRule for Tables and Table Parts

Chapter 5: Tables—InitialStructurePattern and InitialTableFormat

Chapter 6: Inclusions and Exclusions

Chapter 7: AutoInsertions

Chapter 8: Defining and Formatting Objects

Chapter 9: Attribute List

Chapter 10: AllContext formatting rules

Chapter 11: ContextRule formatting rules

Chapter 15: Structuring Unstructured Data

Chapter 1: Getting Started

Introduction

In this module, you will learn how FrameMaker works with structured content models, identify how to get started creating an Element Definition Document, identify the various types of elements you can define and the various parts of an element definition.

Objectives

- Define structured documentation
- Recognize benefit of FrameMaker versus other structured content authoring tools
- Review overall development process
- Identify several ways to create initial EDD
- Identify basic types of elements you can define
- Identify parts of element definition

Understanding How an EDD Controls Structure and Formatting

Structured documents are organized into logical chunks of information, called elements. Elements have rules related to their:

- Content
- Hierarchy
- Order
- Frequency
- Necessity (Required or Optional)

A content model in XML and SGML environments is defined by either a Document Type Definition (DTD) or a Schema. FrameMaker uses a document called an Element Definition Document (EDD) to manage both the content model and the formatting of the content itself.

Authors focus on content and organization of information, not formatting. Focusing on content promotes documentation consistency throughout companies and across industries. Consistency improves communication of information.

In FrameMaker, authors create and edit documents using elements which are:

- Defined in a corresponding EDD
- Imported into design template, creating the **Element Catalog** in the design template. The element catalog, along with other traditional FrameMaker components like master pages and other formatting information make up a structured template.

Ways to create an EDD

There are several ways to create an initial EDD:

- If you are conforming to an existing DTD, you can convert a DTD to an EDD.
- If no DTD exists, but you have a structured FrameMaker document containing an element catalog, you can export the **Element Catalog** as an EDD from your structured document.
- If no DTD and no comparable structured document, you can start with a new, empty EDD.

After a brief review of DTD and EDD files, you'll start in this workbook with a new, empty EDD.

Exercise 1:   Downloading class files

The first few lessons utilize sample files, and later lessons have incremental files available for your use to help keep you aligned with the workbook.

If class files haven't already been downloaded for your use, you'll want to download them before starting the lessons.

To download the lesson files:

1. Open a browser like Chrome or FireFox and navigate to
    https://techcomm.tools/files2019edd

2. Provide your name and email to get the files sent to you via email. A confirmation message will be sent to ensure you've entered the proper address.

3. Answer the confirmation message in the affirmative to receive the file download link for the
    EDD-WB-Files-15-0-3.zip file.

4. Decompress the **EDD-WB-Files-15-0-3**.zip file to your preferred location. Choose a logical location (like the root of the C: drive, your desktop, or your Documents folder) as you'll need to access these files throughout the course.

Exercise 2:   Exploring a raw DTD

In this exercise, you will open a sample DTD, without converting it to an EDD, and view it as a text file.

1. From your
    EDD-WB-Files-15-0-3 directory, open **sample.dtd**.

    a. From the **File** menu, choose **Open**.

        The **Open** dialog appears.

    b. If necessary, change to your class files directory.

    c. If necessary, choose **All Files** (*.*) from the filetype menu.

    d. Double-click **sample.dtd**.

        The **Unknown File Type** dialog appears.

    e. Select **Text** and click **Convert**.

        The **Reading Text File** dialog appears.

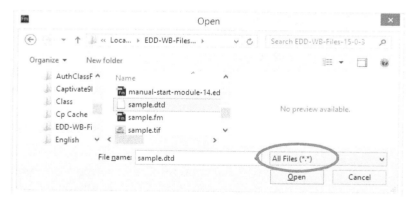

f.   Turn on **Treat Each Line as a Paragraph** and
click **Read**.

The sample DTD appears.

```
<!--DTD for Chapter. Typically invoked by

      <!DOCTYPE  Chapter  SYSTEM "c:\class\SAMPLE.DTD">

-->




<!--Chapter: Chapter is container of all elements within individual chapter of

maintenance manual-->

<!ELEMENT Chapter      - -  (Title, Section, Section+) >

<!ATTLIST Chapter      Author    CDATA      #REQUIRED

                       Version   NUTOKEN    1.0 >

<!ELEMENT Title        - -  (#PCDATA) >

<!ATTLIST Title        ID        ID         #IMPLIED >

<!ELEMENT Section      - -  (Head, (((Para, List?)+, (Section, Section+)?) |

                            (Section, Section+))) >

<!ELEMENT Head         - -  (#PCDATA) >

<!ATTLIST Head         ID        ID         #IMPLIED >

<!ELEMENT List         - -  (Item, Item+) >

<!ATTLIST List         ListType  (Bulleted|Numbered)  Bulleted >

<!ELEMENT Item         - -  (Para+) >

<!ELEMENT Para         - -  (#PCDATA) >
```

2. Scroll through the DTD, viewing its contents.

The text version of the DTD is more like application code, and not very human-friendly.

3. Close the file without saving.

In the next exercise, you will open the DTD and convert it to an EDD, which includes a more readable version of the DTD code.

Exercise 3: Converting a DTD into an EDD

In this exercise, you will open a sample DTD, converting it to an EDD, and view the resulting element definitions.

1. Select
   Structure>DTD > Open DTD.

   The **Open DTD** dialog appears.

2. If necessary, change to your class files directory.

3. Double-click **sample.dtd.**

   The **Use SGML Application** dialog appears.

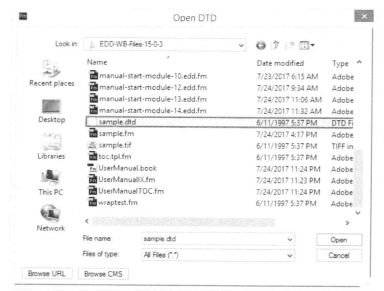

4. Choose **<No Application>** from the **Use Structured Application** popup menu, and click **Continue.**

   The **Select Type** dialog appears.

5. Select **SGML** (if necessary) and select **OK.**

   An alert appears indicating "Finished reading DTD."

6. Click **OK** to dismiss alert.

   An untitled EDD appears with element and attribute definitions corresponding to original DTD.

7. Scroll through the EDD,
    viewing its contents.

    Because, you are
    experimenting with the
    various ways to create an
    EDD, you will not save this
    EDD.

8. Close the file without
    saving.

Next, you will export the
Element Catalog as EDD from a
structured document with
comparable structure.

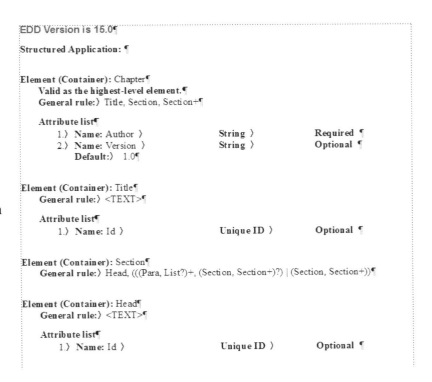

Exercise 4:   Exporting an EDD from a Structured FrameMaker Document

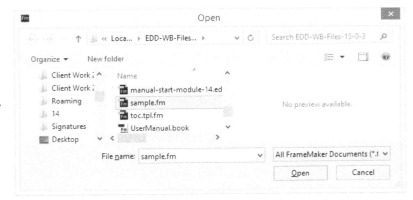

In this exercise, you will export the **Element Catalog** as an EDD from a structured document.

1. From your class files
    directory, open **sample.fm**.

    a. Display the **Open** dialog
        by choosing **File>Open**.

    b. If necessary, change to
        your class files directory.

    c. Double-click **sample.fm**.
        Dismiss any missing
        resource dialogs.

        The sample structured
        document appears.

2. Scroll through the sample document, viewing its contents.

3. Choose **Structure > Structured View** to display the **Structure View** pane.

   The **Structure View** displays the document contents in a hierarchy of elements.

4. Choose **View > Pods > Element Catalog** to display the **Element Catalog**.

   The **Element Catalog** displays the elements available for insertion at your cursor position.

5. Create a new EDD based on the current document's element catalog by choosing **Structure > EDD > Export Element Catalog as EDD**.

Chapter 9[[[]
[Side Doors]]

[[Alice Wong]
[Technical Documentation]
[February 21, 1997]]

9.1 [[INTRODUCTION]

9.1.1 [[Chapter Overview]

9.1.1.1 [[Procedures in This Chapter]
[This chapter describes maintenance procedures for the side doors on the AstroLiner T440B and T442 light rail cars. It includes safety guidelines, an overview of door components, and a maintenance schedule for some of the components.]

[The procedures in this chapter cover disassembling and reinstalling door panels.]]

9.1.1.2 [[Related Information]
[For information about routine operational testing, see Chapter 5 of the manual *[Testing and Troubleshooting]* in this volume, part number [TT1-500 093]. For detailed troubleshooting techniques that address specific side door problems, see Chapter 18 of the same manual.]]]

9.1.2 [[Safety Guidelines]

9.1.2.1 [[Basic Precautions]
[All maintenance personnel must wear approved protective clothing and follow the safety guidelines outlined in the *[Work Safely]* booklet at all times.]]

An untitled EDD appears, with element and attribute definitions corresponding to element catalog of the Sample.fm structured document.

6. Scroll through the EDD, viewing its contents.

   Notice the addition of formatting specifications in this file.

   Because, you are experimenting with the various ways to create an EDD, you will not save this EDD. Next, you will create an EDD from scratch.

7. Close the EDD without saving.

8. Close the **Sample.fm** document without saving.

EDD Version is 15.0

C:\EDD-WB-Files-15-0-3\sample.fm

March 20, 2019

Element (Container): Author
  General rule: <TEXT>

  Text format rules

  1. **In all contexts.**
       Default font properties
       Language: None

Element (Container): BookTitle
  General rule: <TEXTONLY>

  Text format rules

  1. **In all contexts.**
       Text range.
       Use character format: BookTitle

Element (Container): Caption
  General rule: <TEXT>
  Inclusions: IndexEntry, Footnote

  Text format rules

  1. **In all contexts.**
       Use format change list: Head

  2. **In all contexts.**
       Basic properties
          Paragraph spacing
             Change space below by: 12.0 pt

Exercise 5:   Creating a New EDD from Scratch

In this exercise, you will create a new EDD and save it in your Class directory with an appropriate filename.

1. Choose **Structure>EDD> New EDD.**

    The new EDD appears.

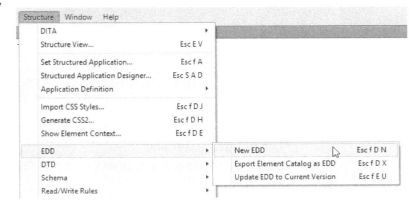

2. If not already open, open the **Structure View** and the **Element Catalog**.

    The **Structure View** displays the elements automatically inserted with any new EDD, with the insertion point to the right of the Tag element bubble. If needed, click to the right of the tag element in the **Structure View**.

    The **Element Catalog** displays **<TEXT>**, prompting you to type the Tag of the first element you are defining.

    Next, you will save the EDD with the appropriate filename and analyze your document type for its structure, the most important step before beginning to define your elements.

3. Use the **Save As** dialog to save the EDD in the directory containing your class files with the new filename, EDD.fm.

    a. From the File menu, choose **Save As**.

        The **Save Document** dialog appears.

    b. If necessary, change to your class files directory.

    c. In the **File name** field, delete the current file name and type: EDD.fm

    d. Click **Save**.

 If you omit the .fm extension, FrameMaker will automatically add it for you.

Visualizing a Content Model

Throughout the EDD development in this training course, you will be acting as the structure developer for the publications department of a fictional metropolitan transit authority. Your task is to ensure that all maintenance manuals written by your department have the same structure. Throughout the next series of exercises, you will:

*   Analyze the document type for its structure

*   Define your elements and attributes in an EDD

*   Test the element definitions by

    -   Importing them into a template

    -   Inserting, wrapping, changing, merging, splitting, unwrapping elements

    -   Inserting and editing attribute values

When you analyze your document type (in this case, maintenance manuals), you draw a diagram of the document's structure, showing:

*   Logical chunks of information, called elements

*   Element hierarchy

*   Element content

*   Element order

*   Notations about frequency about whether the elements are required or optional

*   Attribute information

The structure diagram can be as minimal or as detailed as you want.

Typically, the more analysis done up front, the easier it will be to define your elements.

When analyzing your content:

- Work as a small team to get input from all those involved in using and approving the structure—authors (end users), format designers, structure developers, managers
- Work with a representative sample of the content
- Incorporate any company specifications—structure or style guides
- Analyze from the top down—bigger chunks first, then smaller chunks as needed
- Provide only as much structure as needed—don't over analyze

Exercise 6: Analyzing Your Content

In this exercise, you will analyze your content for its structure, the most important step before beginning to define your elements.

1. Review the sample (the next six pages of this module) of a chapter in the maintenance manual for your fictional organization.

   Normally, you would be viewing many samples of chapters, as well as the entire manual. In this set of materials you will start with something simple and enhance its structure as you go along.

   You will finish by defining an entire book with a table of contents and index by the end of the course.

2. Take out a sheet of paper and take about five minutes to map out a diagram of its structure as you see it, similar to the diagram on page 16 in this module.

Normally, this is an iterative process, involving a team of authors (end users), format designers, structure developers, and managers. It might take hours, if not days or even weeks of revision for more complicated structures.

3. If you are learning this material in a class or course, compare your structure diagram to your neighbor's, noticing the different possibilities for this fairly simple structure. If not, consider how you might alternately represent the content.

4. Compare your structure diagram to the one on page 16, familiarizing yourself with its:

   - Element tags
   - Element hierarchy
   - Element content
   - Element order
   - Notations about frequency and whether the elements are required or optional

Once you're finished with this exercise, review the reference tables at the end of the module. They describe the relationship between different types of elements and their component parts. You may want to refer back to these tables as you go through the material.

Hardcopy Sample for Structure Diagram

Page 1

Chapter 1. Side Doors

1.1. Introduction

1.1.1. Chapter Overview

1.1.1.1. Procedures in This Chapter

This chapter describes maintenance procedures for the side doors on the AstroLiner T440B and T442 light rail cars. It includes safety guidelines, an overview of door components, and a maintenance schedule for some of the components.

The procedures in this chapter cover disassembling and reinstalling door panels.

1.1.1.2. Related Information

For information about routine operational testing, see *Chapter 5 of the manual Testing and Troubleshooting* in this volume, part number TT1-500 093. For detailed troubleshooting techniques that address specific side door problems, see *Chapter 18 of the same manual.*

Page 2

1.1.2. Safety Guidelines

1.1.2.1. Basic Precautions

All maintenance personnel must wear approved protective clothing and follow the safety guidelines outlined in the *Work Safely booklet* at all times.

1.1.2.2. Additional Safety Measures

Additional safety measures must be observed when working on the electrical and pneumatic systems of the side doors. Follow these rules in particular:

+   Turn off all power to high-voltage equipment, and ground all wires before performing maintenance procedures.

+   Always work with your assigned "buddy" or another technician present who can perform CPR or call for aid if necessary.

Some of the procedures in this chapter have warnings regarding the hazards associated with specific tasks. Failure to observe these warnings may result in injury or fatality.

Page 3

1.13. Maintenance Overview

1.13.1. Components of the Side Doors

All AstroLiner T440B and T442 light rail cars have six sets of top-hung side doors. See Figure 1. Components of the side doors, on page 2. Each door set consists of a panel that slides to the right and a panel that slides to the left, operated by a pneumatic door operator.

Each set of doors has its own emergency release unit with a warning bell assembly. Each individual panel has an obstruction-detecting sensitive edge and a bottom brush seal.

Figure 1. Components of the side doors

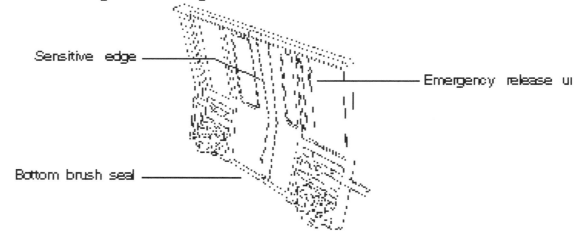

Sensitive edge

Emergency release ui

Bottom brush seal

Page 4

1.1.3.2. Maintenance Schedules

Comprehensive overhaul procedures are scheduled semi-annually. Barring malfunction needing immediate attention, doors are scheduled for weekly operational checks and maintenance is performed as necessary. See Table 1. Items needing routine maintenance, on page 2. The table lists the items that should be checked each week.

Table 1. Items needing routine maintenance

Item	Part number	Per car
Door operator	83-48	4
Emergency release unit	36-95	2
Warning bell assembly	41-91	1
Signal bell assembly	78-90	1
Brush seals	46-94	8

1.1.3.3. Tools and Materials Required

Make sure that you have the following tools and materials before beginning any maintenance tasks.

+ Screwdrivers

Page 5

Flat-head and Phillips-head

+ Adjustable wrenches

+ Approved lubricant—HS 1200 high-speed bearing grease

+ Voltage meter

+ Air pressure gauge

+ Approved blow dryer—Model 390 or 490

1.2. Procedures

1.2.1. Door Panel Removal

1.2.1.1. When to Remove Door Panels

Remove door panels under the following conditions:

+ when a door panel is physically damaged and needs to be replaced or repaired

+ when a panel is jammed and approved techniques for loosening it are unsuccessful

If operations checks indicate that electrical power is not reaching the doors, or that the pneumatic system is not functioning properly, conduct additional tests on the door opera-

Page 6

tor and repair that component as necessary.

1.2.1.2. Procedure

The following procedure applies to removal of one or both door panels on a side door. As you remove the panels place all small parts on clean rags, using one rag for each type of part.

1. Unlock and lift the access panel covering the hanger assembly.

    See Figure 2. Hanger assembly, on page 4. The figure shows a side view of the assembly, without the access panel.

Figure 2. Hanger assembly

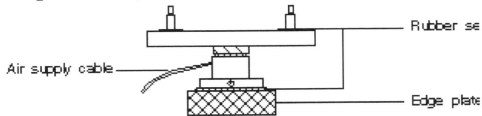

2. Unplug the air supply cable.

3. Loosen and remove the hex nuts and lock washers.

4. Remove the rubber seals.

Structure Diagram

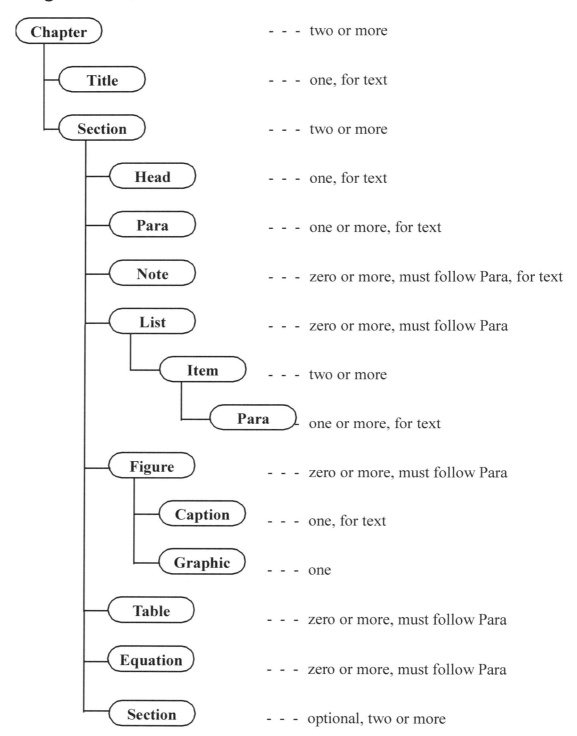

Chapter - - - two or more

Title - - - one, for text

Section - - - two or more

Head - - - one, for text

Para - - - one or more, for text

Note - - - zero or more, must follow Para, for text

List - - - zero or more, must follow Para

Item - - - two or more

Para - one or more, for text

Figure - - - zero or more, must follow Para

Caption - - - one, for text

Graphic - - - one

Table - - - zero or more, must follow Para

Equation - - - zero or more, must follow Para

Section - - - optional, two or more

Relationship between EDD Elements and their component parts

An EDD itself has a content model applied to it. For each type of element defined in an EDD, there are required and optional elements available. The following chart shows which objects allow or require certain other objects within their definition.

	Comments	Tag	Type	ValidHighestLevel	GeneralRule	Inclusion & Exclusion	AutoInsertions	InitialStructurePattern	InitialTableFormat	InitialObjectFormat	SystemVariableFormatRule	AttributeList	TextFormatRules	First/LastParagraphRules	Prefix/SuffixRules
Container	O	R	R	R	R	O	O					O	O	O	O
Table	O	R	R		R	O		O	O			O	O		
TableTitle	O	R	R		R	O						O	O		
TableHeading	O	R	R		R	O		O				O	O		
TableBody	O	R	R		R	O		O				O	O		
TableFooting	O	R	R		R	O		O				O	O		
TableRow	O	R	R		R	O		O				O	O		
TableCell	O	R	R		R	O						O	O		
Footnote	O	R	R		R	O						O	O		
CrossReference	O	R	R							O		O			
Equation	O	R	R							O		O			
Graphic	O	R	R							O		O			
Marker	O	R	R							O		O			
SystemVariable	O	R	R								O	O			

R=Required, O=Optional

Basic Types of Elements You Can Define

Grouping	Type	Purpose
Containers, Tables and Table Parts, Footnotes	**Container**	General-purpose elements for text, child elements, or both
	Table	Parent of entire table
	TableTitle	Contains text for title of table
	TableHeading	Contains 1+ rows
	TableBody	Contains 1+ rows
	TableFooting	Contains 1+ rows
	TableRow	Contains 1+ cells
	TableCell	Contains text and/or child elements
	Footnote	Appears at bottom of column
Objects	**CrossReference**	For referencing other elements
	Equation	For inserting equations
	Graphic	For holding graphics
	Marker	For holding index or other markers
	SystemVariable	For inserting date, filename, or other system variables

Chapter 2: Initial Definition of Your First Element

Introduction

Now that you have created and saved your EDD, you'll need to expand on the rules it will contain.

The following table shows the various parts of an element definition. This module focuses on the preliminary parts: element Tag, Comments, Type, and ValidHighestLevel.

The following list shows the various things an element definition might contain:

- Comments
- Tag
- Type
- ValidHighestLevel
- GeneralRule
- Inclusion & Exclusion
- AutoInsertions
- InitialStructurePattern
- InitialTableFormat
- InitialObjectFormat
- SystemVariableFormatRule
- AttributeList
- TextFormatRules
- First/LastParagraphRules
- Prefix/SuffixRules
- Container

This module focuses on the preliminary parts: the element's **Tag**, **Comments**, **Type**, and **ValidHighestLevel** settings for your Chapter element.

You'll learn about other options for this highest level element and for other elements in subsequent chapters.

Objectives

- Set **Element Catalog** and other options to improve navigation
- Review purpose of preliminary element parts: **Tag**, **Comments**, **Type**, and **ValidHighestLevel**
- Insert the **Element** element
- Type the element **Tag**
- Insert the **Comments** and type a descriptive element comment
- Select the **Type** of element
- Specify that an element is **ValidHighestLevel** in its flow

Setting up your editing environment

Exercise 1:   Opening your EDD

You may still have EDD.fm open from the previous chapter. If not, open it from your class files directory.

If you didn't complete the Chapter 1 exercises, open **Chapter 2-start Initial EDD.fm** from your class files directory and resave it as EDD.fm.

If needed, download the class files by visiting **https://techcomm.tools/files2019edd**

The following two exercises are optional, but will allow you to more rapidly and intuitively complete the remainder of this workbook.

Exercise 2:   Set Element Catalog options

An EDD follows its own content model, so setting the **Element Catalog** to display only the available elements will speed up your entry and will also help you understand the EDD content model itself.

1. In the **Element Catalog**, select the **Settings** button (⚙) to display the **Set Available Elements** dialog.

2. Select the following options:
    *   Valid Elements for Working Start to Finish
    *   List after Other Valid Elements
3. Select the **Set** button.

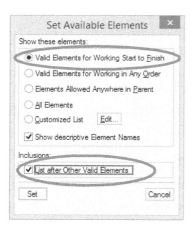

Your element catalog will now show a subset of elements, based on your current location within a document, and will show infrequently used elements (when defined as **Inclusions**) after the more frequently used elements.

Exercise 3:   View Element Boundaries

You may find that navigating within the EDD is easier when viewing the element boundaries. Viewing boundaries allows you to move more accurately within the structure view with your left and right cursor arrows.

1. (if element boundaries are not already visible) Select **View Element Boundaries**.

You should now see square brackets as shown here. If your text symbols are visible, use the **View** menu to turn off paragraph marks, or pilcrows, as they are not useful when working with structured documents and not useful in EDDs in particular.

[Automatically create formats on import.]

[[Element:]]]

Specifying an Element Tag

An element tag is a required part of all element definitions

- An element tag is a descriptive name of an element
- A tag may be up to 255 characters, but better to keep tags concise
- Tags are case-sensitive
- Tags can contain white space
- Characters that perform special functions in SGML or XML are not valid in Tag names. . The following characters will be used within the EDD for other functions, so an element tag cannot contain any of these special characters:

    ( ) & | , * + ? < > % [ ] = ! ; : { } "

 Exercise 4:   Typing the Element Tag

In a new EDD, the first **Element** element and child **Tag** element are inserted automatically.

In this exercise, you will type the **Tag** of the first element, naming it Chapter.

1. Open the file EDD.fm that you created in the previous chapter.
2. In the **Structure View** of the EDD.fm file, click to the right of the **Tag** element.
3. In the Tag element, type: Chapter

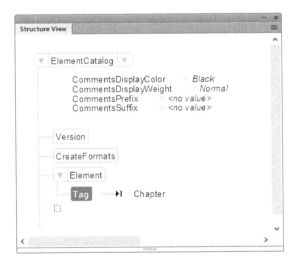

Comments

Optional part of all element definitions

- Allows you to type a description of an element in your own words
- Comments may contain an unlimited number of characters

Exercise 5:   Commenting the Element Definition

In this exercise, you will insert a **Comments** element and add a comment describing your **Chapter** element.

1. In the **Structure View**, click above the **Tag** element, on the line descending from **Element** element.

2. Double-click on the **Comments** element in the **Element Catalog**.

    A **Comments** element appears.

3. In the Comments element, type:

```
Chapter is the container for all elements within chapters of
maintenance manuals
```

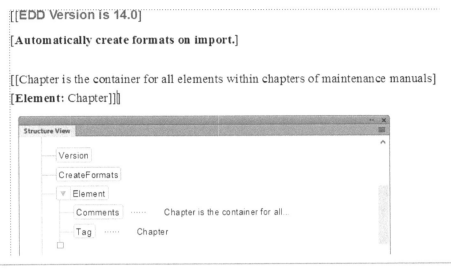

 Prefacing the comment with the tag name is a good idea, since when collapsed, the first characters of the comment (the snippet) displays instead of the tag name.

Element Type

Required part of all element definitions

Some elements match up to special parts, like cross-references or index markers, while many elements simply contain text or other elements. Elements containing text or other elements are generally defined as **Containers**.

Exercise 6:   Identifying the Element as a Container

In this exercise, you will identify **Chapter** as a **Container** element. To do this, click below the **Tag** element, in the **Chapter** element definition.

1. In the **Structure View**, click below the **Tag** element, above the red square beneath the **Element** element.

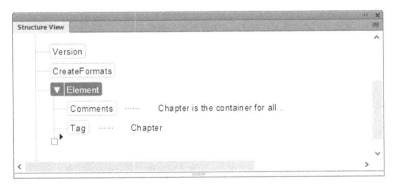

2. From the **Element Catalog**, insert a **Container** element.

   The **Container** element and **GeneralRule** child elements appear automatically.

   If they don't, set the **Element>New Element Options** to Allow Automatic Insertion of Children.

   You'll define the **GeneralRule** in the next chapter.

3. Save your changes.

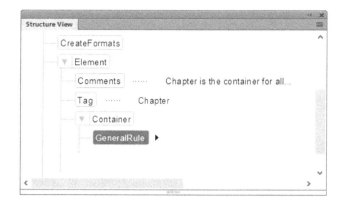

ValidHighestLevel

Required part of element definition for at least one Container element for each structured flow

- Identifies container that holds all elements in flow
- Also required for highest-level element for book files
- **ValidHighestLevel** can appear above or below general rule

Exercise 7: Specifying an element as ValidHighestLevel

In this exercise, you will insert a **ValidHighestLevel** element to define the **Chapter** element as valid at the highest level in its structured flow. A **ValidHighestLevel** element may be placed either above or below a **GeneralRule** element.

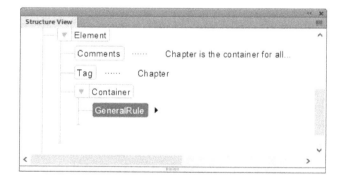

1. In the **Structure View**, click above or below the **GeneralRule** element, on the line descending from the **Container** element.

2. From the **Element Catalog**, insert a **ValidHighestLevel** element.

   A **ValidHighestLevel** element and **Yes** child element appear.

3. Save your changes.

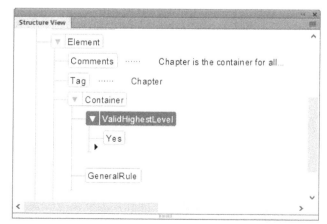

Chapter 3: GeneralRule for Containers and Footnotes

Introduction

This chapter focuses on defining the **GeneralRule** for **Container** elements and **Footnote** elements.

Objectives

- Write **GeneralRule** for **Container** elements and **Footnote** elements
- Use occurrence indicators and connectors in a **GeneralRule**
- Use content symbols and parentheses in a **GeneralRule**
- Review default **GeneralRule** for **Container** and **Footnote** elements
- Import the EDD into the structured template
- Test element definitions in the structured template

Overview

Elements defined in your EDD must be referenced in at least one general rule.

Elements referenced in a general rule must be defined in your EDD.

General rules are a required part of element definitions for:

- Containers
- Table, TableTitle, TableHeading, TableBody, TableFooting, TableRow, TableCell elements
- Footnotes

General rules specify:

- The child elements allowable in an element
- Whether child elements are required or optional
- The frequency in which child elements can occur
- The order in which child elements can occur
- Whether element may contain <TEXT>

Syntax

Occurrence indicators allow you to specify whether a child:

- Is required or optional
- Can be repeated

Here are the occurrence indicators allowable in a general rule:

Symbol	Meaning
Question mark (?)	Child is optional and can occur once
Asterisk (*)	Child is optional and can occur more than once
Plus sign (+)	Child is required and can occur more than once
NONE	Child is required and must occur only once

Connectors

You can use connectors to:

- Separate multiple element tags in **GeneralRule**
- Specify order of child elements

Here are the connectors allowable in a general rule:

Symbol	Meaning
Comma (,)	Child elements must occur in order given
Ampersand (&)	Child elements can occur in any order
Vertical bar (|)	Any one of child elements in group can occur

Grouping

You can use parentheses to:

- Define groups of element tags
- Define groups within groups

   All connectors in group of element tags must be of the same type

Special Content Types

You can use content strings to:

- Specify content other than child elements
- Indicate elements with no content

String	Meaning
<TEXT>	Can contain text and any inclusions
<TEXTONLY>	Can contain only text Cannot contain child elements, even inclusions defined in ancestors' content rules
<ANY>	Can contain any combination of text and elements defined in EDD
<EMPTY>	Cannot contain any text or elements

GeneralRule and Element Catalog Import Defaults

Effect of importing an empty GeneralRule

If you import an EDD with an empty GeneralRule element into template, FrameMaker will insert a default GeneralRule.

Here are the default rules entered for containers and footnotes:

Element Type	Default GeneralRule
Container	<ANY>
Footnote	<ANY>

After defining element definitions in the EDD, you import the element definitions into your structured template. If the template has no Element Catalog, FrameMaker creates new Element Catalog for template. If the template has existing Element Catalog, FrameMaker replaces old Element Catalog.

Testing EDD Changes

After importing element definitions into a structured document you should test your changes.

To test the definitions, you:

- Insert and wrap variety of elements in document
- Make sure automatic child elements appear as defined
- Move elements around in document, checking Structure View to see that elements are valid only where they should be
- Enter attribute values in elements that allow them
- Check Structure View to make sure that kinds of values you want to add are valid according to attribute's definition
- Move elements around to verify that they are formatted correctly according to context
- Verify that extra formatting items such as prefixes and autonumbers appear as defined

Iterative Testing

After testing the element definitions in the structured template you may need to revise definitions in your EDD, reimport, test, and repeat as necessary.

Writing the GeneralRule for a Highest Level Element

Exercise 1:   Writing a GeneralRule Using Occurrence Indicators and Connectors

In this exercise, you will define the **GeneralRule** for the **Chapter** element's contents, as one **Title** element, following by two or more **Section** elements.

1. If it is not already open, open `EDD.fm`, from the directory containing your class files.

    If you didn't complete the previous chapter exercises, open up the
    Chapter 3-start Containers.fm file in your class directory and save it as `EDD.fm` in your class files directory.

If needed, download the class files by visiting **https://techcomm.tools/files2019edd**

2. In the **Structure View**, click to the right of the
    GeneralRule element.

3. In the GeneralRule element, type:
    `Title, Section, Section+`

    Commas specify an explicit order. Spaces aren't essential but are helpful for readability.

    You might interpret this rule as "A valid chapter must contain a title, followed by a section, followed by one or more optional sections" or "A valid chapter must contain a title, followed by two or more sections."

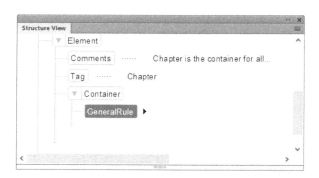

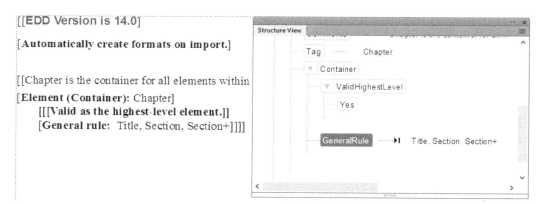

4. Save your changes.

Having referenced Title and Section, you now need to define these elements.

Exercise 2:   Writing a GeneralRule using the <TEXT> building block

In this exercise, you will define the **Title** element, by:

- Inserting an **Element** element and typing the **Tag** as **Title**
- Inserting a **Container** element to specify **Title** as a container
- Typing the **GeneralRule** for the **Title** element's contents: **<TEXT>**

To add your title element, do the following:

1. In the **Structure View**, click at the end of your EDD, below the **Element** element for the **Chapter** tag, on the line descending from the **ElementCatalog** element.

2. From the **Element Catalog**, insert an **Element** element.

    The **Element** element and **Tag** child element appear automatically.

3. With the insertion point to the right of the **Tag** element, type: `Title`

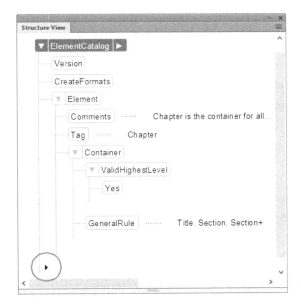

4. Click below the **Tag** element, above the red square beneath the **Element** element.

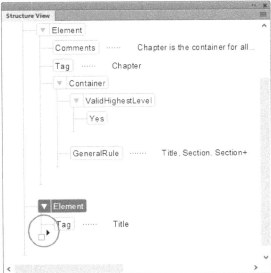

5. From the **Element Catalog**, insert **Container.**

    The **Container** element and **GeneralRule** child element appear.

6. With the insertion point to the right of the **GeneralRule** element, type: <TEXT>

7. Save your changes.

 At this point you may want to start collapsing the previous elements to improve navigation in the **Structure View.**

Exercise 3:   Defining Another Container of Child Elements

In this exercise, you will define the **Section** element, by:

- Inserting an **Element** element and typing the **Tag** as **Section**
- Inserting a **Container** element to specify **Section** as a container
- Typing the **GeneralRule** for the **Section** element's contents: one **Head** element followed by one or more **Para** elements

To define your section element, do the following:

1. In the **Structure View**, click below the **Title** element definition, on the line descending from the **ElementCatalog** element.

2. From the **Element Catalog**, insert an **Element** element.

    The **Element** element and **Tag** child elements appear.

3. With the insertion point to the right of the **Tag** element, type: Section

4. Click below the **Tag** element, above the red square at the end of the **Element** element.

5. From the **Element Catalog**, insert **Container**.

   The **Container** element and **GeneralRule** child element appear.

6. With the insertion point to the right of the GeneralRule element, type: `Head, Para+`

   The + indicates that Para is required, and can occur more than once.

7. Save your changes.

Next, you'll define these two newly specified elements.

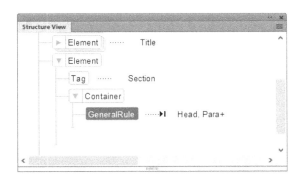

Exercise 4:   Defining More Descendant Container Elements

In this exercise, you will define the **Head** and **Para** elements, by:

- Inserting an **Element** element and typing the **Tag** as `Head`
- Inserting a **Container** element to specify **Head** as a container
- Typing the **GeneralRule** for the **Head** element's contents: <TEXT>
- Inserting another **Element** element and typing the **Tag** as Para
- Inserting a **Container** element to specify **Para** as a container
- Typing the **GeneralRule** for the **Para** element's contents: <TEXT>

To insert your new elements, do the following:

1. Insert another **Element** element and tag it **Head**.

   a. In the **Structure View**, click below the **Element** element (for the **Section** tag), on the line descending from the **ElementCatalog** element.

   b. From the **Element Catalog**, insert an **Element** element.

      The **Element** element and **Tag** child element appear.

   c. In the **Tag** element, type: `Head`

2. Define **Head** as a **Container** with a **GeneralRule** of <TEXT>

   a. Click below the **Tag** element.

   b. From the **Element Catalog**, insert **Container**.

      The **Container** element and **GeneralRule** child element appear.

   c. In the **GeneralRule** element, type: <TEXT>

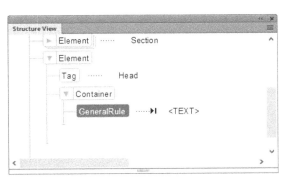

3. Insert another **Element** element and tag it `Para`.

   a. In the **Structure View**, click below the last **Element** element.

   b. From the **Element Catalog**, insert an **Element** element.

   An **Element** element and a **Tag** child element appear.

   c. In the **Tag** element, type: `Para`

4. Define **Para** as a **Container** with a **GeneralRule** of <TEXT>

   a. Click below the **Tag** element.

   b. From the **Element Catalog**, insert **Container**.

   Container element and **GeneralRule** child element appear.

   c. In the **GeneralRule** element, type: `<TEXT>`

5. Save your changes.

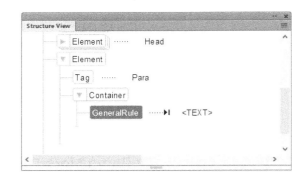

Importing and Testing

Exercise 5: Importing the EDD

In this exercise, you will create a new portrait document, save it as your structured template, then import the element definitions defined in the EDD into your structured template.

1. Create a new portrait document.

   a. Select **File > New > Document**.

   The **New** dialog box appears.

   b. Click **Portrait**.

   A new blank document appears.

2. Use the **Save As** dialog box to save the new portrait document in your class files directory with the new filename `testdoc.fm`.

   a. From the File menu, choose **Save As**.

   The Save Document dialog box appears.

   b. If necessary, change to your class files directory.

   c. In the Save in File text box, delete the current file name and type: `testdoc.fm`

   d. Click **Save**.

3. Ensure that `testdoc.fm` is the active file and choose **File > Import > Element Definitions**.

   The **Import Element Definitions** dialog box appears.

4. From the **Import from Document** popup menu, choose EDD.fm.

The EDD must be open, else it will not appear in the menu.

5. Click **Import**.

   An alert appears indicating completion of the
   import process.

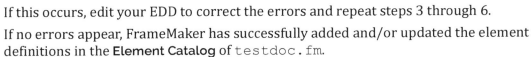

6. Click **OK** to close the alert box.

7. If errors exist in the element definitions, a log file
   (separate window) might appear identifying the
   problems.

   If this occurs, edit your EDD to correct the errors and repeat steps 3 through 6.

   If no errors appear, FrameMaker has successfully added and/or updated the element
   definitions in the **Element Catalog** of testdoc.fm.

8. Save your changes.

Exercise 6: Testing the EDD

In this exercise, you will test your **Chapter**, **Title**, **Section**, **Head**, and **Para** element definitions by
inserting elements and typing text into elements defined to contain text.

1. Choose **View>Element Boundaries**.

   This will display the square brackets around content once you've added elements to your
   document.

2. If not open already, open the **Element Catalog** and **Structure View**.

3. Set available elements to
   Valid Elements for Working Start to Finish.

   a. Choose **Element>Set Available Elements**.

      The **Set Available Elements** dialog box appears.

   b. In **Show Tags For**, turn on **Valid Elements for Working Start to
      Finish**.

   c. In **Inclusions**, choose **List after Other Valid Elements**.

   d. Click **Set**.

      The **Element Catalog** displays only the **Chapter** element as
      the element valid at the highest level in the structure.

      If you don't see **Chapter** in the **Element Catalog**, click inside
      of the text frame in the Document Window.

4. From the **Element Catalog**, insert a **Chapter** element.

   The **Structure View** displays the **Chapter** element bubble, the **Document Window** displays element boundaries for the **Chapter** element, and the **Element Catalog** displays an available **Title** child element.

5. Insert a **Title** element.

   The **Element Catalog** displays **<TEXT>**, indicating that you can type in this element.

6. In the **Title** element, type:
   ```
   Title of Chapter in
   Maintenance Manual
   ```

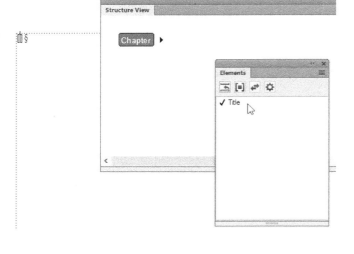

7. Click below the **Title** element and insert a **Section** element.

   The **Element Catalog** updates to reflect the new position of your cursor within the document.

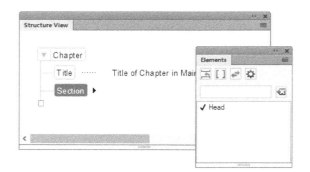

8. Insert a **Head** element and type:
   ```
   Heading for First Section
   ```

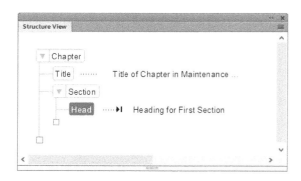

9. Click below the **Head** element, insert a **Para** element, and type: `Text for first paragraph within Section.`

10. Click below the **Para** element and insert several more **Para** elements to verify that you can insert more than one **Para** element.

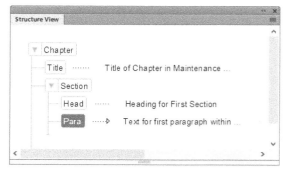

11. Notice the square hole on the line descending from the **Chapter** element.

    That's because **Chapter** is required to have two or more **Section** elements.

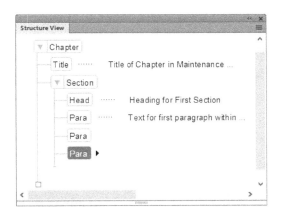

12. Insert another Section element, one Head, and 2 Para elements.

    Don't bother to type any more text. You are just testing, and you have already made sure that you can type in these elements when you inserted them in the first Section.

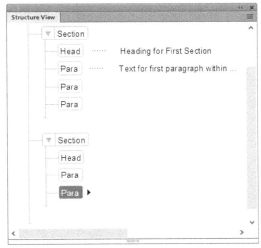

13. Insert a third Section element to verify that you can insert more than two Section elements.

14. Save your changes.

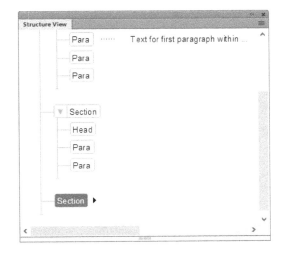

Adding to the EDD, Reimporting and Testing

Exercise 7:   Referencing an Element Using Parentheses in a GeneralRule

In this exercise, you will redefine the **Section** element's **GeneralRule** to allow:

- A mandatory **Head** element followed by a mandatory **Para** element followed by an optional **WarnNote** element

- Optional multiple **Para** and **WarnNote** elements, as long as a **WarnNote** is preceded by a **Para** element

Then, you will define the WarnNote element, by:

- Inserting an **Element** element and giving it a **Tag** of `WarnNote`

- Inserting a **Container** element to specify **WarnNote** as a container

- Typing the **GeneralRule** for the **WarnNote** element's contents: `<TEXT>`

To modify your general rule, do the following:

1. In the EDD, locate the element definition for the **Section** element.

2. In the **Document Window**, change the **GeneralRule** as follows:

    `Head, (Para, WarnNote?)+`

    The newly referenced **WarnNote** element will require a definition.

3. Insert another **Element** element and tag it **WarnNote**.

    a. In the **Structure View**, click below the last **Element** element.

    b. From the **Element Catalog**, insert an **Element** element.

        An **Element element** and a **Tag** child element appear.

    c. In the **Tag** element, type: `WarnNote`

4. Define **WarnNote** as a **Container** with a **GeneralRule** of <TEXT>

    a. Click below the **Tag** element.

    b. From the **Element Catalog**, insert **Container**.

        Container element and **GeneralRule** child element appear.

    c. In the **GeneralRule** element, type: `<TEXT>`

You can use Copy/Paste to speed creation of similar structure.

---

5. Save your changes.

Exercise 8:   Referencing a Group Within a Group

In this exercise, you will redefine the **Section** element's **GeneralRule** to contain:

- A **Head** element, followed by a **Para** element, followed by optional **WarnNote** or **List** elements
- The option of multiple **Para**, **WarnNote** and **List** elements, with the requirement that a **Para** must always precede a **WarnNote** or **List**

Then, you will define the **List** element and its children, by:

- Inserting an **Element** element and typing the **Tag** as List
- Inserting a **Container** element to specify **List** as a **Container**
- Typing the **GeneralRule** for the **List** element's contents: two or more **Item** elements
- Inserting another **Element** element and typing the **Tag** as **Item**
- Inserting a **Container** element to specify **Item** as a **Container**
- Typing the **GeneralRule** for the **Item** element's contents: <TEXT>

To modify the Section general rule, do the following:

1. In the EDD, locate the element definition for the **Section** element.

2. In the **Document Window**, change the **GeneralRule** as follows:

   ```
   Head, (Para, (WarnNote | List)?)+
   ```

   [[**Element (Container):** Section]
       [[**General rule:** Head, (Para, (WarnNote | List)?)

3. Insert another **Element** element and tag it **List**.

   a. In the **Structure View**, click below the last **Element** element.

   b. From the **Element Catalog**, insert an **Element** element.

      An **Element element** and a **Tag** child element appear.

   c. In the **Tag** element, type: List

4. Define **List** as a **Container** with a **GeneralRule** of Item, Item+

   a. Click below the **Tag** element.

   b. From the **Element Catalog**, insert **Container**.

      A **Container** element and **GeneralRule** child element appear.

   c. In the **GeneralRule** element, type: Item, Item+

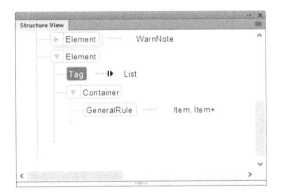

5. Insert another **Element** element and tag it **Item**.

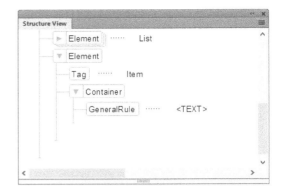

a. In the **Structure View**, click below the last **Element** element.

b. From the **Element Catalog**, insert an **Element** element.

An **Element element** and a **Tag** child element appear.

c. In the Tag element, type: `Item`

6. Define **Item** as a **Container** with a **GeneralRule** of <TEXT>

a. Click below the **Tag** element.

b. From the **Element Catalog**, insert **Container**.

Container element and **GeneralRule** child element appear.

c. In the **GeneralRule** element, type: <TEXT>

7. Save your changes.

 ### Exercise 9:   Reimporting and Retesting

In this exercise, you will reimport the EDD into the structured template and test your element definitions for **Section**, **WarnNote**, **List**, and **Item**.

1. Reimport your element definitions and fix any errors.

a. In `testdoc.fm`, from the **File** menu, choose **Import > Element Definitions**.

The **Import Element Definitions** dialog box appears.

b. From the **Import** from **Document** popup menu, choose `EDD.fm`.

c. Click **Import**.

An alert box appears indicating "**Element definitions have been imported from the EDD**"

d. Click **OK** to close the alert box.

e. If you had errors in the element definitions, a log file (separate window) appears identifying the problems. Edit your EDD and reimport until the errors are resolved.

 If you did not have errors, a log file will not appear and you do not need to edit your EDD and reimport before testing.

FrameMaker replaces element definitions in the **Element Catalog** of the structured template.

2. In the **Structure View**, click on the line descending from any **Section** element but below a **Para** element.

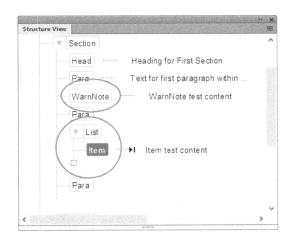

3. From the **Element Catalog**, insert a **WarnNote** element and type any text to test it.

4. Click on the line descending from any **Section** element but below a **Para** element.

5. Insert a **List** element.

6. In the **List** element, insert an **Item** element and type any text to test it.

7. Notice the red square on the line descending from the **List** element.

   A **List** must have two or more **Item** elements to conform to the content model.

8. Insert several more **Item** elements to verify that you can have as many as needed.

9. Try inserting two consecutive **WarnNote** elements.

   Upon insertion of the second element a red square appears between the elements. This indicates that other content (in this case, a Para) is needed between two consecutive **WarnNote** elements.

10. Try inserting two consecutive **List** elements.

    Upon insertion of the second element a red square appears between the elements. This indicates that other content (in this case, a Para) is needed between two consecutive **List** elements.

11. Try inserting a **List** immediately after a **WarnNote**, or vice versa.

    Upon insertion of the second element a red square appears between the elements. This indicates that other content (in this case, a Para) is needed between **List** and **WarnNote** elements.

12. Try inserting a **List** after a **Head**.

    Upon insertion of the second element a red square appears between the elements. This indicates that other content (in this case, a Para) is needed between **Head** and **List** elements.

13. Save your changes.

Exercise 10: Referencing an Element Within Itself

In this exercise, you will redefine the **Section** element's **GeneralRule** to contain a **Head** element followed by either:

- Repeatable **Para** element with optional **WarnNote** and **List** elements, followed by two or more optional **Section** elements

- Or just two or more **Section** elements without preceding **Para**, **WarnNote**, and **List** elements

To do this:

1. In the EDD, locate the element definition for the **Section** element.

2. In the Document Window, change the **GeneralRule** as follows:

   [[**Element (Container):** Section]
       [[**General rule:** Head, (((Para, (WarnNote | List)?)+, (Section, Section+)?) |
           (Section, Section+))]]]

   ```
   Head, (((Para, (WarnNote | List)?)+, (Section, Section+)?) |
   (Section, Section+))
   ```

3. Save your changes.

4. Reimport your element definitions and fix any errors.

   a. In `testdoc.fm`, from the **File** menu, choose **Import > Element Definitions**.

   Import Element Definitions dialog box appears.

   b. From the **Import from Document** popup menu, choose `EDD.fm`.

   c. Click **Import**.

   An alert box appears indicating "**Element definitions have been imported from the EDD**"

   d. Click **OK** to close the alert box.

   e. If you had errors in the element definitions, edit your EDD and reimport.

5. Practice inserting **Section** elements.

   Whenever you insert a **Section** element, you must insert two or more at the same level, and they must be the last two children of their parent.

6. Save your changes.

Exercise 11: Referencing and Defining a Footnote Element

In this exercise, you will redefine the **Para** element's **GeneralRule** to contain:

- <TEXT> or a **Footnote** element
- With the option of repeating the choice any number of times

Then, you will define the **Footnote** element, by:

- Inserting an **Element** element and typing the **Tag** as **Footnote**
- Inserting a **Footnote** element to specify **Footnote** as a footnote
- Typing the **GeneralRule** for the **Footnote** element's contents: <TEXT>

To define a footnote element, do the following:

1. In the EDD, locate the element definition for the **Para** element.

2. In the **Document Window**, change the **GeneralRule** as follows:

   `(<TEXT> | Footnote)+`

   > [[**Element (Container):** Para]
   >   [[**General rule:** (<TEXT> | Footnote)+]]]

   The newly referenced footnote element will eventually need to be defined as an actual footnote structure, but for now we'll just define it as a container. Later you'll redefine the footnote to be able to take advantage of the footnote functionality already available within FrameMaker.

3. Insert another **Element** element and tag it **Footnote**.

   a. In the **Structure View**, click below the last **Element** element.

   b. From the **Element Catalog**, insert an **Element** element.

      An **Element element** and a **Tag** child element appear.

   c. In the **Tag** element, type: `Footnote`

4. Define **Footnote** as a **Footnote** with a **GeneralRule** of <TEXT>

   a. Click below the **Tag** element.

   b. From the **Element Catalog**, insert **Footnote**.

      Footnote element and **GeneralRule** child element appear.

   c. In the **GeneralRule** element, type: <TEXT>

5. Save your changes.

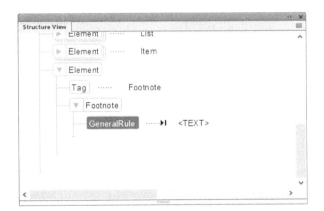

6. Reimport your element definitions and fix any errors.

    a. In `testdoc.fm`, from the **File** menu, choose **Import > Element Definitions**. **Import Element Definitions** dialog box appears.

    b. From the **Import from Document** popup menu, choose `EDD.fm`.

    c. Click **Import**.

    An alert box appears indicating "**Element definitions have been imported from the EDD**"

    d. Click **OK** to close the alert box.

    e. If you had errors in the element definitions, edit your EDD and reimport.

7. In the **Structure** View, click on the line descending from any **Section** element.

8. From the **Element Catalog**, insert a **Para** element and type any text to test it.

9. With your insertion point still in the text, insert a **Footnote** element and type any text to test it.

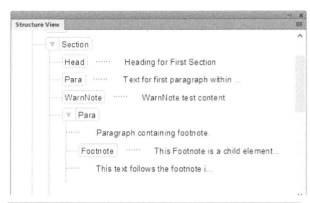

10. Click below the Footnote element, on the line descending from the Para element, and type a little more text.

11. With your insertion point still in the text, insert another **Footnote** element and type any text to verify that you can insert multiple **Footnote** elements in a **Para** element.

12. Try inserting a **Footnote** element in a **Head** element.

    You cannot. In your EDD, **General Rules** are currently written so that **Footnote** elements can be children of **Para** elements, not **Head** or other elements.

13. Save your changes.

Chapter 4: GeneralRule for Tables and Table Parts

Introduction

This chapter focuses on defining the **GeneralRule** for **Table** elements and table part elements.

Objectives

- Write **GeneralRule** for **Table** element
- Write **GeneralRule** for table part elements—**TableTitle, TableHeading, TableBody,** TableFooting, TableRow, TableCell
- Review default **GeneralRules**
- Review restrictions on **GeneralRules** for **Table** and table part elements
- Reimport the EDD into the structured template
- Test **Table** and table part element definitions in the structured template

Overview

A General Rule is a required part of element definitions for:

- Container
- Table, TableTitle, TableHeading, TableBody, TableFooting, TableRow, TableCell
- Footnote

The GeneralRule specifies:

- Child elements that an element can contain
- Whether child elements are required or optional
- Frequency in which child elements can occur
- Order in which child elements can occur
- Whether element can have <TEXT>

Syntax

Occurrence indicators permit you to specify whether a child:

- Is required or optional
- Can be repeated

Symbol	Meaning
Question mark (?)	Child is optional and can occur once
Asterisk (*)	Child is optional and can occur more than once
Plus sign (+)	Child is required and can occur more than once
NONE	Child is required and must occur only once

Use connectors to:
- Separate multiple element tags in GeneralRule
- Specify order of child elements

Symbol	Meaning
Comma (,)	Child elements must occur in order given
Ampersand (&)	Child elements can occur in any order
Vertical bar (|)	Any one of child elements in group can occur

Use parentheses to:
- Define groups of element tags
- Define groups within groups

    All connectors in group of element tags must be of the same type

Use content symbols to:
- Specify content other than child elements
- Indicate element with no content

Symbol	Meaning
<TEXT>	Can contain text and any inclusions
<TEXTONLY>	Can contain only text Cannot contain child elements, even inclusions defined in ancestors' content rules
<ANY>	Can contain any combination of text and elements defined in EDD
<EMPTY>	Cannot contain any text or elements

GeneralRule Restrictions

Element type	Restrictions
Table	• One each of TableTitle, TableHeading, TableBody, TableFooting (in that order) • TableBody required • TableTitle, TableHeading, TableFooting optional • No plus sign (+), asterisk (*), ampersand (&) • No <TEXT>, <TEXTONLY>, <ANY>, <EMPTY>
TableTitle	• All child elements are allowed, except Table and table parts • <TEXT>, <TEXTONLY>, <ANY>, <EMPTY> allowed
TableHeading	• One or more TableRow child elements • No <TEXT>, <TEXTONLY>, <ANY>, <EMPTY>
TableBody	• One or more TableRow child elements • No <TEXT>, <TEXTONLY>, <ANY>, <EMPTY>
TableFooting	• One or more TableRow child elements • No <TEXT>, <TEXTONLY>, <ANY>, <EMPTY>
TableRow	• One or more TableCell child elements • No <TEXT>, <TEXTONLY>, <ANY>, <EMPTY>
TableCell	• All child elements are allowed, except Table and table parts • <TEXT>, <TEXTONLY>, <ANY>, <EMPTY> allowed

Default GeneralRule

If you import EDD with an empty GeneralRule element into template. FrameMaker inserts a default GeneralRule:

Element Type	Default GeneralRule
Table	TITLE?, HEADING?, BODY, FOOTING?
TableTitle	<ANY>
TableHeading	ROW+
TableBody	ROW+
TableFooting	ROW+
TableRow	CELL+
TableCell	<ANY>

Referencing and Defining the Table Element

Exercise 1:   Referencing a Table Element in a GeneralRule

In this exercise, you will redefine the **Section** element's **GeneralRule** to contain optional **PartsTable** elements.

1. If it is not already open, from your class files directory, open EDD.fm, the EDD you've been modifying throughout the class.

If you did not finish the previous chapter's modifications to the EDD, please open **Chapter 4-start Tables.fm** instead, and save it in your class files directory as `EDD.fm`.

 If needed, download the class files by visiting
https://techcomm.tools/files2019edd

2. In the EDD, locate the element definition for the **Section** element.

3. In the **Document Window**, change the **GeneralRule** as follows:

[[**Element (Container)**: Section]
    [[**General rule**: Head, (((Para, (WarnNote | List | PartsTable)?)+, (Section, Section+)?) | (Section, Section+))]]]

```
Head, (((Para, (WarnNote | List | PartsTable)?)+,
(Section, Section+)?) | (Section, Section+))
```

4. Save your changes.

 ### Exercise 2:   Defining a Table Element

In this exercise, you will define the **PartsTable** element, by:

- Inserting an **Element** element and typing the **Tag** as **PartsTable**
- Inserting a **Table** element to specify **PartsTable** as a table
- Typing the **GeneralRule** for the **PartsTable** element's contents: **TableTitle** element, followed by **TableHeading** element, followed by **TableBody** element, followed by optional **TableFooting** element

Although FrameMaker requires only that a table have a body of one row with one cell, you will put tighter restrictions on your table by using structure. You will:

- Require the **TableTitle**
- Require the **TableHeading**

In subsequent exercises, you will put even tighter restrictions on your table. You will:

- Allow only <TEXT> in the **TableTitle**.
- Allow only one row in the required **TableHeading**, although FrameMaker allows any number.
- Allow only one row in the optional **TableFooting**, although FrameMaker allows any number.
- Allow only 3 columns (by specifying three cell children for the row element), although FrameMaker allows any number.
- Allow only <TEXT> in the cells.

To define the **PartsTable** element:

1. Insert a new **Element** element and tag it **PartsTable**.

    a. In the **Structure View**, click below the last **Element** element.

    b. From the **Element Catalog**, insert an **Element** element.

       An **Element** element and **Tag** child element appear.

    c. In the **Tag** element, type: `PartsTable`

2. Define **PartsTable** as a **Table** with a **GeneralRule** of TableTitle, TableHeading, TableBody, TableFooting?

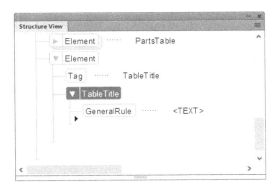

   a. Click below the **Tag** element.

   b. From the **Element Catalog**, insert **Table**.

   c. A **Table** element and **GeneralRule** child element appear.

   d. In **GeneralRule** element, type:
   ```
   TableTitle, TableHeading, TableBody, TableFooting?
   ```

3. Save your changes.

Next you will define the new table parts you referenced in this rule.

Defining Table Part Elements

Exercise 3: Defining a TableTitle Element

In this exercise, you will define the **TableTitle** element, by:

- Inserting an **Element** element and typing the **Tag** as **TableTitle**
- Inserting a **TableTitle** element to specify **TableTitle** as a table title
- Typing the **GeneralRule** for the **TableTitle** element's contents: <TEXT>

To define the **TableTitle** element:

1. Insert another **Element** element and tag it **TableTitle**.

   a. In the **Structure View**, click below the last **Element** element.

   b. From the **Element Catalog**, insert an **Element** element.

   An **Element** element and a **Tag** child element appear.

   c. In the Tag element, type: TableTitle

2. Define **TableTitle** as a **TableTitle** with a **GeneralRule** of <TEXT>

   a. Click below the **Tag** element.

   b. From the **Element Catalog**, insert **TableTitle**.

   A **TableTitle** element and a **GeneralRule** child element appear.

   c. In the **GeneralRule** element, type: <TEXT>

3. Save your changes.

Exercise 4: Defining a TableHeading Element

In this exercise, you will define the **TableHeading** element, by:

- Inserting an **Element** element and typing the **Tag** as **TableHeading**
- Inserting a **TableHeading** element to specify **TableHeading** as a table heading

- Typing the **GeneralRule** for the **TableHeading** element's contents: one **PartRow** element

To define the **TableHeading** element:

1. Insert another **Element** element and tag it **TableHeading**.

   a. In the **Structure View**, click below the last **Element** element.

   b. From the **Element Catalog**, insert an **Element** element.

      An **Element** element and a **Tag** child element appear.

   c. In the **Tag** element, type: `TableHeading`

2. Define **TableHeading** as a **TableHeading** with a **GeneralRule** of **PartRow**.

   a. Click below the **Tag** element.

   b. From the **Element Catalog**, insert **TableHeading**.

      TableHeading element and **GeneralRule** child element appear.

   c. In the **GeneralRule** element, type: `PartRow`

3. Save your changes.

You'll define the PartRow later, after defining a few other elements.

Exercise 5:   Defining a TableBody Element

In this exercise, you will define the **TableBody** element, by:

- Inserting an **Element** element and typing the **Tag** as **TableBody**
- Inserting a **TableBody** element to specify **TableBody** as a table body
- Typing the **GeneralRule** for the **TableBody** element's contents: one or more **PartRow** elements

To define the **TableBody** element:

1. Insert another **Element** element and tag it **TableBody**.

   a. In the **Structure View**, click below the last **Element** element.

   b. From the **Element Catalog**, insert an **Element** element.

      An **Element** element and a **Tag** child element appear.

   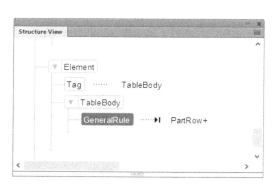

   c. In the **Tag** element, type: `TableBody`

2. Define **TableBody** as a **TableBody** with a **GeneralRule** of **PartRow+**

   a. Click below the **Tag** element.

   b. From the **Element Catalog**, insert **TableBody**.

      TableBody element and **GeneralRule** child element appear.

   c. In the **GeneralRule** element, type: `PartRow+`

3. Save your changes.

Exercise 6:   Defining a TableFooting Element

In this exercise, you will define the **TableFooting** element, by:

- Inserting an **Element** element and typing the **Tag** as **TableFooting**
- Inserting a **TableFooting** element to specify **TableFooting** as a table footing
- Typing the **GeneralRule** for the **TableFooting** element's contents: one **PartRow** element

To define the **TableFooting** element:

1. Insert another **Element** element and tag it **TableFooting**.

   a. In the **Structure View**, click below the last **Element** element.

   b. From the **Element Catalog**, insert an **Element** element.

   An **Element** element and a **Tag** child element appear.

   c. In the **Tag** element, type: `TableFooting`

2. Define **TableFooting** as a **TableFooting** with a **GeneralRule** of **PartRow**.

   a. Click below the **Tag** element.

   b. From the **Element Catalog**, insert **TableFooting**.

   TableFooting element and **GeneralRule** child element appear.

   c. In the **GeneralRule** element, type: `PartRow`

3. Save your changes.

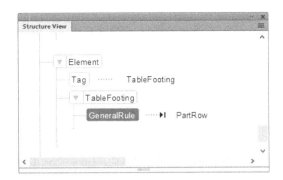

Exercise 7:   Defining a TableRow Element

In this exercise, you will define the **PartRow** element, by:

- Inserting an **Element** element and typing the **Tag** as **PartRow**
- Inserting a **TableRow** element to specify **PartRow** as a table row
- Typing the **GeneralRule** for the **PartRow** element's contents: one **PartName**, one **PartNum**, one **PartCount**

To define the **PartRow** element:

1. Insert another **Element** element and tag it **PartRow**.

   a. In the **Structure View**, click below the last **Element** element.

   b. From the **Element Catalog**, insert an **Element** element.

   An **Element** element and a **Tag** child element appear.

   c. In the **Tag** element, type: `PartRow`

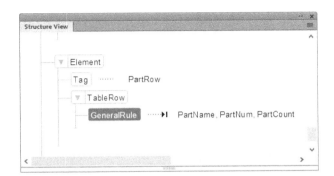

2. Define **PartRow** as a **TableRow** with a **GeneralRule** of **PartName**, **PartNum**, **PartCount**.

   a. Click below the **Tag** element.

   b. From the **Element Catalog**, insert **TableRow**.

   A **TableRow** element and **GeneralRule** child element appear.

   c. In the **GeneralRule** element, type: `PartName, PartNum, PartCount`

3. Save your changes.

Exercise 8:   Defining TableCell Elements

In this exercise, you will define the PartName, PartNum, and PartCount elements, by:

- Inserting an **Element** element and typing the **Tag** as **PartName**
- Inserting a **TableCell** element to specify **PartName** as a table cell
- Typing the **GeneralRule** for the **PartName** element's contents: <TEXT>
- Repeating the process for **PartNum** and **PartCount**

To define the **TableCell** elements:

1. Insert another **Element** element and tag it **PartName**.

   a. In the **Structure View**, click below the last **Element** element.

   b. From the **Element Catalog**, insert an **Element** element.

   An **Element** element and a **Tag** child element appear.

   c. In the Tag element, type: `PartName`

2. Define **PartName** as a **TableCell** with a **GeneralRule** of <TEXT>

   a. Click below the **Tag** element.

   b. From the **Element Catalog**, insert **TableCell**.

   A **TableCell** element and a **GeneralRule** child element appear.

   c. In the **GeneralRule** element, type: <TEXT>

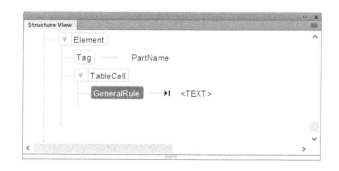

3. Insert another **Element** element and tag it **PartNum**.

   a. In the **Structure View**, click below the last **Element** element.

   b. From the **Element Catalog**, insert an **Element** element.

   An **Element** element and a **Tag** child element appear.

   c. In the Tag element, type: `PartNum`

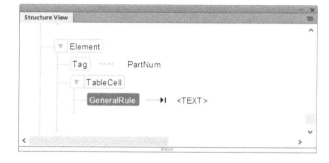

Consider using **Copy/Paste** for duplicating similar structure

4. Define **PartNum** as a **TableCell** with a **GeneralRule** of <TEXT>

   a. Click below the **Tag** element.

   b. From the **Element Catalog**, insert **TableCell**.

      A **TableCell** element and a **GeneralRule** child element appear.

   c. In the **GeneralRule** element, type: <TEXT>

5. Insert another **Element** element and tag it **PartCount**.

   a. In the **Structure View**, click below the last **Element** element.

   b. From the **Element Catalog**, insert an **Element** element.

      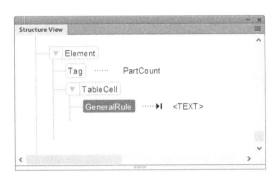

      An **Element** element and a **Tag** child element appear.

   c. In the **Tag** element, type: PartCount

6. Define **PartCount** as a **TableCell** with a **GeneralRule** of <TEXT>

   a. Click below the **Tag** element.

   b. From the **Element Catalog**, insert **TableCell**.

      A **TableCell** element and a **GeneralRule** child element appear.

   c. In the **GeneralRule** element, type: <TEXT>

7. Save your changes.

Reimport and Testing

 Exercise 9:   Reimporting and Testing the Table

In this exercise, you will reimport the EDD into the structured template and test your element definitions for Section and PartsTable.

1. Reimport your element definitions into your test document and fix any errors.

   a. In testdoc.fm, from the **File** menu, choose **Import > Element Definitions**.

      The **Import Element Definitions** dialog appears.

   b. From the **Import** from **Document** popup menu, choose EDD.fm.

   c. Click **Import**.

      An alert box appears indicating "**Element definitions have been imported from the EDD**"

   d. Click **OK** to close the alert box.

   e. If you had errors in the element definitions, edit your EDD and reimport.

2. In the **Structure View**, click on the line descending from any **Section** element but after a **Para** element.

3. From the **Element Catalog**, insert a **PartsTable** element.

   The **Insert Table** dialog appears.

4. In the **Insert Table** dialog, specify:

   - Columns: 3
   - Body Rows: 3
   - Heading Rows: 1
   - Footing Rows: 1

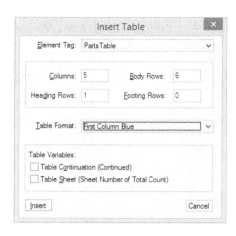

5. Click **Insert**.

   The **Document Window** shows the table.

[Para preceding table]

Table 1:		

[Para after table]]

The **Structure View** shows the table's overall structure, based on the number of rows and columns you specified.

Notice the invalid structure of the **PartRow** elements which all contain three **PartName** elements, not **PartName**, **PartNum**, **PartCount** as defined in the EDD.

By default, FrameMaker uses the first child element (**PartName**) in the **PartRow GeneralRule** and repeats that child element to create all the columns you specify in the **Insert Table** dialog.

Later, you will change this behavior by specifying an **InitialStructurePattern** for **PartRow**. In the meantime, you will change the **PartRow**'s child elements into the correct child elements.

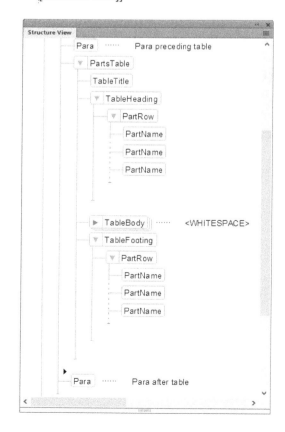

6. Change the **PartName** elements to **PartNum** elements where appropriate.

   a. In the **Structure View**, select the second **PartName** element in the first **PartRow** in the **TableHeading**.

   b. From the **Element Catalog**, select **PartNum** and click **Change**.

   PartName changes to **PartNum**.

   c. Repeat for each additional **PartRow** in the **TableBody** and in the **TableFooting**.

7. Change the **PartName** elements to **PartCount** elements where appropriate.

   a. In the **Structure View**, select the second **PartName** element in the first **PartRow** in the **TableHeading**.

   b. From the **Element Catalog**, select **PartCount** and click **Change**.

   PartName changes to **PartCount**.

   c. Repeat for each additional **PartRow** in the **TableBody** and in the **TableFooting**.

8. Save your changes.

Exercise 10: Testing the Parts of the Table

In this exercise, you will continue testing the parts of the **PartsTable**—TableTitle, TableBody, TableHeading, TableFooting, PartRow, PartName, PartNum, PartCount.

1. In the **Structure View**, click to the right of the **Table 1:** heading and type:

   ```
   Items needing routine maintenance
   ```

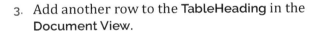

2. Click in at least one of each—**PartName**, **PartNum**, and **PartCount**— and enter text.

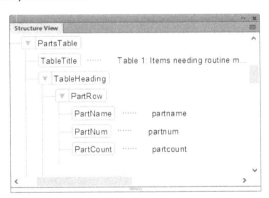

3. Add another row to the **TableHeading** in the **Document View**.

   a. Click in the heading row of the table.

   b. Press **Control-Return**.

   A second PartRow is added to TableHeading, but only one is allowed so the structure shows as invalid.

4. From the **Edit** menu, choose **Undo**.

   The invalid **PartRow** disappears.

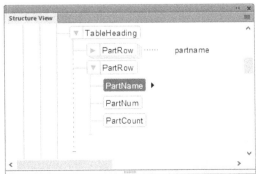

5. Delete the **TableHeading**.

    a. In the **Structure View**, select the **TableHeading** element.

    b. Press **Delete**.

        The Clear Table Cells dialog appears.

    c. Turn on **Remove Cells from Table**.

    d. Click **Clear**.

        The table heading is deleted.

        A TableHeading is required, so the structure is invalid.

6. From the Edit menu, choose **Undo**.

7. Add another row to the TableFooting.

    a. Click in the footing row of the table.

    b. Press **Control-Return**.

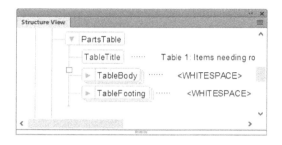

        A second **PartRow** is added to **TableFooting**, but as with the TableHeading, only one is allowed so the structure is invalid.

8. From the **Edit** menu, choose **Undo**.

    The invalid **PartRow** disappears.

9. Delete the **TableFooting** element.

    a. In the **Structure View**, select the **TableFooting** element.

    b. Press **Delete**.

        The **Clear Table Cells** dialog appears.

    c. Turn on **Remove Cells from Table**.

    d. Click **Clear**.

        The **TableFooting** disappears, and the structure is valid because the **TableFooting** is optional.

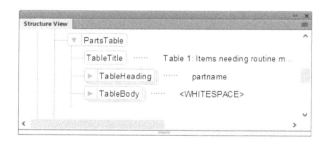

10. Save your changes.

Chapter 5: Tables—InitialStructurePattern and InitialTableFormat

Introduction

This chapter focuses on the **InitialStructurePattern** and **InitialTableFormat** for tables.

Objectives

- Specify **InitialStructurePattern** for **Table** and table part elements
- Specify **InitialTableFormat** for **Table** element
- Reimport and test **InitialStructurePattern** and **InitialTableFormat**

Overview of InitialStructurePattern

InitialStructurePattern is an optional part of element definitions for the following elements:

- Table
- TableHeading
- TableBody
- TableFooting
- TableRow

All tables have these common characteristics:

- Tables have at least a body
- Table heading, body, or footing elements have at least one row
- Table rows have same number of cells as columns in table

When you insert a Table element:

- You use **Insert Table** dialog to specify number of rows in heading, body, footing and number of columns
- FrameMaker automatically inserts necessary child elements to build a basic structure

If you do not specify initial structure, FrameMaker:

- Uses a default **GeneralRule** to give new table or table part its default initial structure
- Builds default initial structure by taking first of each type of table part in table's **GeneralRule**

You can use an InitialStructurePattern to specify:

- The **TableTitle, TableHeading, TableBody, TableFooting** elements that will initially appear in the table element
- The **TableRow** type elements that will appear in the **TableHeading, TableBody, TableFooting** type elements
- The **TableCell** type elements that will appear in the **TableRow** type elements

Specifying an InitialStructurePattern

 ## Exercise 1: Specifying the InitialStructurePattern for a TableRow Element

In this exercise, you will define an **InitialStructurePattern** within the **PartRow** that will insert **PartName, PartNum, PartCount** instead of inserting all **PartName** elements.

1. If it is not already open, from your class files directory, open `EDD.fm`, the EDD you'll be modifying throughout the class.

    If you did not finish the previous chapter's modifications to the EDD, please open **Chapter 5-start Initial Table Format.fm** instead, and save it in your class files directory as `EDD.fm`.

If needed, download the class files by visiting
https://techcomm.tools/files2019edd

---

2. In the EDD, locate the **PartRow** element definition.

3. In the **Structure View**, click below **PartRow's** **GeneralRule** element.

4. From the **Element Catalog**, insert **InitialStructurePattern**.

    An **InitialStructurePattern** element appears.

5. In the **InitialStructurePattern** element, type: `PartName, PartNum, PartCount`

6. Save your changes.

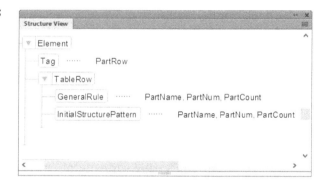

InitialTableFormat—Overview

InitialTableFormat is an optional part of a Table element definition.

- It identifies which table format is preselected in the **Insert Table** dialog when user inserts **Table** element

- If no **InitialTableFormat** specified, **Table** element uses **Format A**

- Make sure table format is consistent with **GeneralRule** for **Table** element

    If **Table** element's **GeneralRule** does not specify a **TableTitle** element, table format should not have one

- **InitialTableFormat** is only a suggestion—user can change to another format without creating format override

You can specify a table format with a(n):

- **AllContextsRule**—wherever the element appears

- **ContextRule**—when element is in certain context

- **LevelRule**—when element is nested a specified number of levels in a specified ancestor

Specifying the InitialTableFormat

Exercise 2: Specifying the InitialTableFormat With an AllContextsRule

In this exercise, you will specify which table format will be preselected in the **Insert Table** dialog when the user inserts the **PartsTable** elements. The user can select a different table format without incurring a format rule override.

1. In the EDD, locate the **PartsTable** element definition.

2. In the **Structure View**, click below **PartsTable's GeneralRule** element.

3. From the **Element Catalog**, insert **InitialTableFormat**.

   An **InitialTableFormat** element appears.

   At this point, you could specify a context-specific or level-specific rule. Since these rules are covered in the next chapter, you will insert a more simple **AllContextsRule**.

4. Insert **AllContextsRule**.

   An **AllContextsRule** element appears.

5. Insert **TableFormat**.

   A **TableFormat** element appears.

6. In the **TableFormat** element, type:
   `Format B`

7. Save your changes.

Reimporting and Testing

Exercise 3: Reimporting/Testing InitialStructurePattern and InitialTableFormat

In this exercise, you will reimport the EDD into the structured template and test your **InitialStructurePattern** on **PartRow** and **InitialTableFormat** on **PartsTable**.

1. Reimport your element definitions and fix any errors.

   a. In `testdoc.fm`, from the **File** menu, choose **Import > Element Definitions**.

      The **Import Element Definitions** dialog appears.

   b. From the **Import from Document** dropdown menu, choose `EDD.fm`.

   c. Click **Import**.

      An alert box appears indicating "**Element definitions have been imported from the EDD**"

   d. Click **OK** to close the alert box.

   e. If you had errors in the element definitions, edit your EDD and reimport.

2. In the **Structure View**, click below a **List** element.

3. From the **Element Catalog**, insert a **Para** element.

4. Click below the **Para** element.

5. Insert a **PartsTable** element.

   The **Insert Table** dialog appears, with **Format B** preselected as you defined in the EDD.

6. In the **Insert Table** dialog, specify:

   - Columns: 3
   - Body Rows: 3
   - Heading Rows: 1
   - Footing Rows: 1

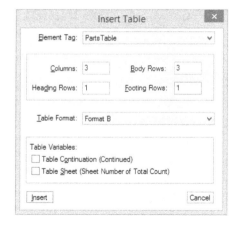

7. Click **Insert**.

   The **Document Window** displays the table.

The **Structure View** displays the table's overall structure, based on the number of rows and columns you specified.

Notice the valid structure of the **PartRow** elements which now contain **PartName**, **PartNum**, **PartCount** as defined in the EDD, rather than three **PartName** elements.

By default, FrameMaker uses the first child element found in the **PartRow GeneralRule** (**PartName** in this case) and repeats that child element to create all the columns you specify in the **Insert Table** dialog. You changed this behavior by specifying an **InitialStructurePattern** for **PartRow**.

8. Save your changes.

Chapter 6: Inclusions and Exclusions

Introduction

This chapter focuses on defining **Inclusions** and **Exclusions** for **Container**, **Footnote**, **Table** and table part elements.

Objectives

- Specify use of an inclusion
- Define the included element
- Specify an exclusion of an element
- Reimport and test inclusions and exclusions

Defining Inclusions

Inclusions are an optional part of element definitions for:

- Containers
- Table, TableTitle, TableHeading, TableBody, TableFooting, TableRow, TableCell
- Footnotes

Inclusions allow elements to occur anywhere inside a defined element or its descendants. They are often used for infrequently used elements that might be necessary in multiple places within the hierarchy, such as **Footnote** or **Term**.

Inclusions greatly simplify the general rules for elements. They also help your audience manage their **Element Catalog** view by listing less critical elements at the bottom of the list of available elements. The **TextRange** element in the screen capture to the right displays the inclusion icon (↲)and is listed after other valid elements via the **Element Catalog Options** (⚙)

Exercise 1: Specifying Inclusions

In this exercise, you will define a new **Container** element tagged **TextRange** to contain the names of other documents mentioned throughout the chapters of the maintenance manuals. Rather than referencing **TextRange** in the **GeneralRule** for each element, you will define it as an inclusion for **Section**. **TextRange** can then be included anywhere within **Section** and its descendants.

1. If it is not already open, from your class files directory, open **EDD.fm**, the EDD you've been modifying throughout the class.

   If you did not finish the previous chapter's modifications to the EDD, please open **Chapter 6-start Inclusions Exclusions.fm** instead, and save it in your class files directory as `EDD.fm`.

If needed, download the class files by visiting
https://techcomm.tools/files2019edd

2. In the EDD, insert another **Element** element and tag it **TextRange**.

   a. In the **Structure View**, click below the last **Element** element.

   b. From the **Element Catalog**, insert an **Element** element.

   An **Element** element and **Tag** child element appear.

   c. In the **Tag** element, type: **TextRange**

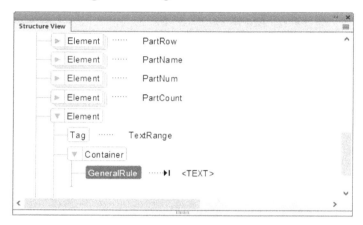

3. Define **TextRange** as a **Container** with a **GeneralRule** of <TEXT>

   a. Click below the **Tag** element.

   b. From the **Element Catalog**, insert **Container**.

   A **Container** element and **GeneralRule** child element appear.

   c. In the **GeneralRule** element, type: <TEXT>

4. In the **Structure View**, locate the **Section** element.

5. Click below the **Section**'s **GeneralRule** element.

6. From the **Element Catalog**, insert **Inclusion**.

   An **Inclusion** element appears.

7. In the **Inclusion** element, type: `TextRange`

8. Save your changes.

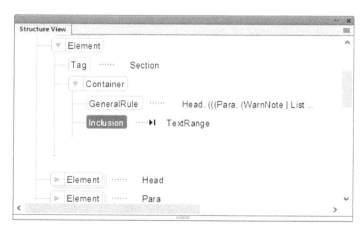

You'll test this change after also defining an exclusion.

Defining Exclusions

Exclusions are an optional part of element definitions for:

- Container
- Table, TableTitle, TableHeading, TableBody, TableFooting, TableRow, TableCell
- Footnote

Exclusions specify:

- Elements that cannot occur anywhere in a defined element or its descendants
- Exclusions are often used to negate inclusions

Exercise 2: Specifying Exclusions

In this exercise, you will exclude **TextRange** from **Head** and **PartsTable** so that it cannot appear within any **Head** element or any **PartsTable** element or its descendant parts.

1. In the **Structure View**, locate the **Head** element definition.

2. Click below the **Head's GeneralRule** element.

3. From the **Element Catalog**, insert **Exclusion**.

   An **Exclusion** element appears.

4. In the Exclusion element, type:
   `TextRange`

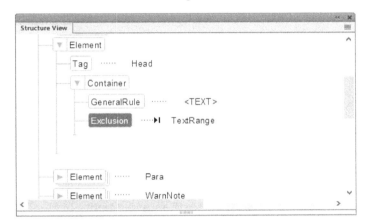

5. In the **Structure View**, locate the **PartsTable** element.

6. Click below the **PartsTable's GeneralRule** element.

7. From the **Element Catalog**, insert **Exclusion**.

   An **Exclusion** element appears.

8. In the **Exclusion** element, type:
   `TextRange`

9. Save your changes.

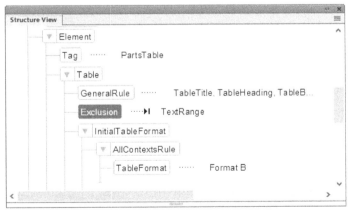

Reimporting and Testing Inclusions and Exclusions

Exercise 3: Reimporting and Testing Inclusions and Exclusions

In this exercise, you will reimport the EDD into the structured template and test your **TextRange** element and inclusions and exclusions.

1. Reimport your element definitions and fix any errors.

   a. In `testdoc.fm`, from the **File** menu, choose **Import > Element Definitions**.

61

The **Import Element Definitions** dialog appears.

   b. From the **Import from Document** popup menu, choose `EDD.fm`.

   c. Click **Import**.

      An alert box appears indicating "**Element definitions have been imported from the EDD**"

   d. Click **OK** to close the alert box.

   e. If you had errors in the element definitions, edit your EDD and repeat this step.

2. In the **Structure View**, click anywhere on the line descending from the **Chapter** element.

    The **Element Catalog** does not show **TextRange** as an inclusion, because you defined it as an inclusion on **Section**, not **Chapter**.

3. Click in the **Title** element.

    The **Element Catalog** does not show **TextRange** as an inclusion, because you defined it as an inclusion on **Section**, and **Title** is a child of **Chapter**, not **Section**.

4. Click anywhere on the line descending from the **Section** element.

    The **Element Catalog** shows **TextRange** as an inclusion.

5. From the **Element Catalog**, insert an **TextRange** element and insert some text.

6. Insert an **TextRange** element in a Para element.

   a. Click in any Para element.

   b. Insert an **TextRange** element.

   c. Type some text.

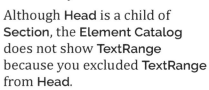

Notice that the **TextRange** element forces a line break in the **Para** element. Later, you will define the **TextRange** element's formatting as a text range, rather than a paragraph, and the break will disappear.

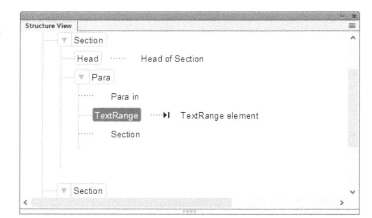

7. Click in any **Head** element.

    Although **Head** is a child of **Section**, the **Element Catalog** does not show **TextRange** because you excluded **TextRange** from **Head**.

8. Click in any **PartNum** element (in the table).

    Although **PartNum** is a descendant of **Section**, the **Element Catalog** does not show **TextRange**, because you excluded **TextRange** from **PartsTable** (**PartsTable** is ancestor of **PartNum**).

9. Save your changes.

Chapter 7: AutoInsertions

Introduction

This chapter focuses on defining element **AutoInsertions** for **Container** elements.

Objectives

- Specify autoinserted child elements
- Specify autoinserted nested child elements
- Reimport and test the AutoInsertions

Overview of Autoinsertions

Autoinsertions are an optional part of element definitions for Container elements only

- They identify a child element to be inserted automatically with its parent
- Autoinsertions can also identify nested children ("grandchild" then "great-grandchild," etc.) to insert automatically
- Autoinsertions cannot automatically insert sibling elements

FrameMaker opens dialogs and windows as needed to specify:

- Attributes
- Table number of rows and columns
- Graphic positioning
- Cross-reference source
- Variable selection
- Marker text

Specifying Autoinserted Child Elements

 Exercise 1:   Specifying Autoinserted Title Element

In this exercise, you will specify that the **Title** child element will appear automatically when you insert the **Chapter** element. When a first child element is required, specifying it as an **AutoInsertion** speeds up the authoring process.

1. If it is not already open, from your class files directory, open `EDD.fm`, the EDD you've been modifying throughout the class.

    If you did not finish the previous chapter's modifications to the EDD, please open **Chapter 7-start AutoInsertions.fm** instead, and save it in your class files directory as `EDD.fm`.

> If needed, download the class files by visiting
> **https://techcomm.tools/files2019edd**

2. In the EDD, locate the **Chapter** element definition.

3. Click below the **Chapter**'s **GeneralRule** element (or click below the **ValidHighestLevel** element if you inserted it below, rather than above, the **Chapter**'s **GeneralRule**).

4. From the **Element Catalog**, insert **AutoInsertions**.

    An **AutoInsertions** element with **InsertChild** element appear.

5. In the **InsertChild** element, type: `Title`

6. Save your changes.

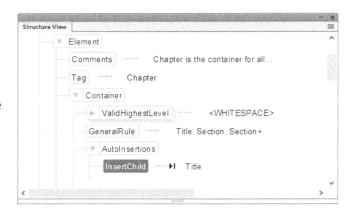

 Exercise 2:   Specifying Autoinserted Head Element

In this exercise, you will specify that the **Head** child element will appear automatically when you insert the **Section** element.

1. In the EDD, locate the **Section** element definition.

2. Click below the **Section**'s **Inclusion** element.

3. From the **Element Catalog**, insert **AutoInsertions**.

    An **AutoInsertions** element with **InsertChild** element appear.

4. In the **InsertChild** element, type: `Head`

5. Save your changes.

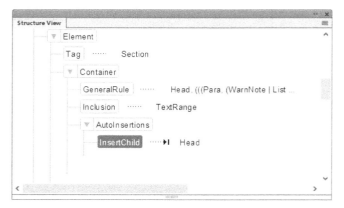

Exercise 3:   Reimporting and Testing Autoinserted Child Elements

In this exercise, you will reimport the EDD into the structured template, verify that **Allow Automatic Insertion of Children** is turned on, and test your **AutoInsertions** on **Chapter** and **Section**.

1. Reimport your element definitions and fix any errors.

    a. In `testdoc.fm`, from the File menu, choose **Import > Element Definitions**.

    The **Import Element Definitions** dialog appears.

    b. From the **Import from Document** popup menu, choose `EDD.fm`.

    c. Click **Import**.

    An alert box appears indicating "**Element definitions have been imported from the EDD**"

    d. Click **OK** to close the alert box.

    e. If you had errors in the element definitions, edit your EDD and reimport.

2. Verify that **Allow Automatic Insertion of Children** is turned on.

    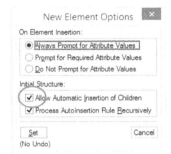

    Although **AutoInsertions** are defined in the EDD, the feature can be turned on and off in the document.

    a. Select **Element>New Element Options**.

    The **New Element Options** dialog appears.

    b. If not already on, turn on **Allow Automatic Insertion of Children**.

    c. Click **Set**.

3. In the **Structure View**, select and delete the **Chapter** element.

    Since **Chapter** is the highest-level element, all your test content disappears. (Yes, this is what you need to do!)

4. From the **Element Catalog**, insert a **Chapter** element.

    The **Chapter** element appears, but this time is followed by a **Title** child element, courtesy of the **InsertChild** element in your EDD.

    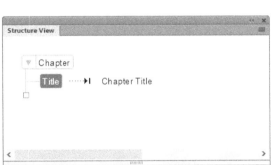

5. Type sample content into the **Title** element.

6. Click below the **Title** element.

7. Insert a **Section** element.

    A **Section** element appears, along with a child element of **Head**.

8. Type sample content into the **Head** element.

9. Save your changes.

Specifying Autoinserted Child and Nested Child Elements

Exercise 4: Specifying Autoinserted Item and Nested Para Elements

In this exercise, you will redefine the **Item** element to contain one or more **Para** elements with optional **WarnNote** elements, rather than just <TEXT>. (In a later exercise, you will define formatting so that "first" and "not first" **Para** elements in Item elements have different formatting.)

After redefining **Item**, you will specify **AutoInsertions**:

- List will automatically insert **Item** child and **Para** nested child
- **Item** will automatically insert **Para** child

1. In the EDD, locate the **Item** element definition.

2. In the **Document Window**, replace the **GeneralRule** as follows:

   ```
   (Para, WarnNote?)+
   ```

This general rule now allows more than one paragraph of text to be inserted into an **Item** element.

3. In the **Structure View**, locate the **List** element definition.

4. Click below the **List's GeneralRule** element.

5. From the **Element Catalog**, insert **AutoInsertions**.

   AutoInsertions element with **InsertChild** element appear.

6. In the **InsertChild** element, type: `Item`

7. Click below the **InsertChild** element.

8. From the **Element Catalog**, insert **InsertNestedChild**.

   An **InsertNestedChild** element appears.

9. In the **InsertNestedChild** element, type: `Para`

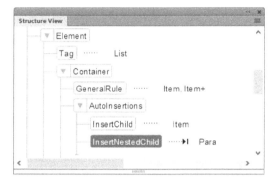

   Now, when you insert a **List** element, an **Item** child element and a nested **Para** child element will appear. However, this does not mean that when you insert an additional **Item** element, its **Para** child element will appear. To do this you will need to define an **Item** autoInsertion separately.

10. In the **Structure View**, locate the **Item** element definition.

11. Click below the **Item's GeneralRule** element.

12. From the **Element Catalog**, insert **AutoInsertions**.

    An **AutoInsertions** element with **InsertChild** element appear.

13. In the **InsertChild** element, type: `Para`

14. Save your changes.

Reimporting and Testing Item and Para Autoinsertions

Exercise 5: **Reimporting and Testing Autoinserted Nested Child Elements**

In this exercise, you will reimport the EDD into the structured template and test your AutoInsertions on List and Item.

1. Reimport your element definitions and fix any errors.

   a. In `testdoc.fm`, from the File menu, choose **Import > Element Definitions**.

      Import Element Definitions dialog appears.

   b. From the **Import from Document** popup menu, choose `EDD.fm`.

   c. Click **Import**.

      An alert box appears indicating "**Element definitions have been imported from the EDD**"

   d. Click **OK** to close the alert box.

   e. If you had errors in the element definitions, edit your EDD and repeat this step.

2. In the **Structure View**, click below the **Head** element.

3. From the **Element Catalog**, insert a **Para** element.

4. Click below the **Para** element.

5. Insert a **List** element.

   List element and **Item** child element and **Para** nested child element appear.

6. Click below the **Item** element, on the line descending from the **List** element.

7. Insert an **Item** element.

   Item element and **Para** child element appear.

8. Save your changes.

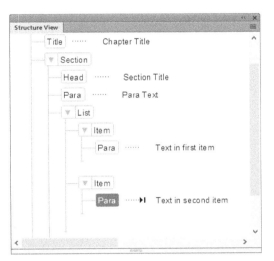

Chapter 8: Defining and Formatting Objects

Introduction

This chapter focuses on defining objects like cross-references, equations, graphics, and markers. These types of elements usually require formatting, using things like the InitialObjectFormat and the SystemVariableFormatRule for system variables.

Objectives

- Define a CrossReference type element
- Specify the InitialObjectFormat of a cross-reference, referring to a cross-reference format stored in a document
- Define an Equation type element
- Specify the InitialObjectFormat of an equation, referring to equation size
- Define a Graphic type element
- Specify the InitialObjectFormat of a graphic, using the Import File or Anchored Frame dialog
- Define a Marker type element
- Specify the InitialObjectFormat of marker, referring to the marker type
- Define a SystemVariable type element
- Specify the SystemVariableFormatRule, referring to variable name
- Reimport and test object elements and formats

Overview of InitialObjectFormat

The InitialObjectFormat is an optional part of an object's element definition and specifies the default formatting applied when inserting an object.

Object	InitialObjectFormat
CrossReference	Name of cross-reference format stored in the documents to be preselected in Cross-Reference dialog when user inserts element
Equation	Equation size of Small, Medium or Large
Graphic	ImportedGraphicFile or AnchoredFrame
Marker	Marker type to be preselected in Insert Marker dialog when user inserts element

The InitialObjectFormat is only a suggestion—an author can choose another format without creating format override.

If InitialObjectFormat is not specified, FrameMaker applies defaults as follows:

Object	InitialObjectFormat
CrossReference	Last Cross-Reference format chosen in dialog
Equation	Medium
Graphic	AnchoredFrame
Marker	Last marker type chosen in Insert Marker dialog or Marker window

There are a number of ways to specify an InitialObjectFormat. You can specify a format with:

- AllContextsRule—wherever the element appears
- ContextRule—when element is in certain context
- LevelRule—when element is nested a specified number of levels in a specified ancestor

CrossReference Elements

Exercise 1:   Defining a CrossReference and InitialObjectFormat

In this exercise, you will:

- Redefine the Para element to contain optional XRef elements
- Define the XRef element as a CrossReference, using the InitialObjectFormat of ElemNumTextPage

The InitialObjectFormat for the XRef means that the ElemNumTextPage will be preselected in the Cross-Reference dialog when the user inserts the XRef elements. The user can select a different cross-reference format without incurring a format rule override.

1. If it is not already open, from your class files directory, open EDD.fm, the EDD you've been modifying throughout the class.

    If you did not finish the previous chapter's modifications to the EDD, please open Chapter 8-start Define Format Objects.fm instead, and save it in your class files directory as EDD.fm.

If needed, download the class files by visiting https://techcomm.tools/files2019edd

2. In the EDD, locate the Para element definition.

3. In the Document Window, change the GeneralRule as follows:

    (<TEXT> | Footnote | **XRef**)+

[[Element (Container): Para]
    [[**General rule:** (<TEXT> | Footnote | XRef)+]]]

4. Insert another Element element and tag it XRef.

    a. In the Structure View, click below the last Element element.

    b. From the Element Catalog, insert an Element element.

        An Element element and a child element appear.

    c. In the Tag element, type: XRef

5. Define XRef as a CrossReference.

    a. Click below the Tag element.

    b. From the Element Catalog, insert CrossReference.

        A CrossReference element appears.

6. From the Element Catalog, insert InitialObjectFormat.

    InitialObjectFormat element appears.

7. Insert AllContextsRule.

    AllContextsRule element appears.

8. Insert CrossReferenceFormat.

    CrossReferenceFormat element appears.

9. In the CrossReferenceFormat element, type: `ElemNumTextPage`

10. Save your changes.

Exercise 2:   Reimporting and Testing the Cross-Reference Element

In this exercise, you will reimport the EDD into the structured template and test your element definitions for Para and XRef.

1. Reimport your element definitions and fix any errors.

    a. In `testdoc.fm`, from the File menu, choose Import > Element Definitions.

        Import Element Definitions dialog appears.

    b. From the Import from Document popup menu, choose `EDD.fm`.

    c. Click Import.

        An alert box appears indicating "Element definitions have been imported from the EDD"

    Element Catalog Manager Report

    March 25, 2019 10:54 am
    Imported EDD: C:\EDD-WB-Files-15-0-3\EDD.fm
    Destination Document:

    d. Click OK to close the alert box.

        Because the format ElemNumTextPage does not exist, a

    Messages…
    Creating new cross-reference format (ElemNumTextPage).

    Element Catalog Manager completed.

    log file appears, indicating that the format is being created for you. You will define this format to meet your needs later in this exercise.

    e. Close the log file without saving it.

2. In the Structure View, click in any Para element.

3. From the **Element Catalog**, insert an **XRef** element.

   If not already visible, the **Cross-Reference** pod appears with **ElemNumTextPage** preselected from the **Format** popup menu. The format was created for you on import, but the format's definition (displayed below the format name, circled in the screencapture) is blank.

   Next, you will edit the definition.

4. Click **Edit Format**.

   The **Edit Cross-Reference Format** dialog appears.

5. In the **Definition** text box, type:
   ```
   See <$elemparanum> <$elemtext>,
   on page <$elempagenum>.
   ```

6. Click **Change** to change the format.

   Note: Adding a leading space to a cross-reference format allows you to omit a leading space when inserting full-sentence cross-references.

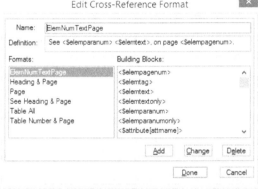

7. Click **Done** to dismiss the **Edit Cross-Reference Format** dialog.

   The **Update References** dialog appears.

8. Click **Update** to update any references that have been inserted using the format.

   Note that the **Cross-Reference** pod is empty.

   Before you can successfully insert an element-based cross-reference, you need to define some attributes for the **XRef** element and the elements that will be referenced. You will do that in a later module. After adding attributes to your content model, you will be able to insert cross-references to **Title**, **Head**, **Figure**, and **PartsTable** elements.

9. Save your changes.

   Note: In your own work, consider storing the format of ElemNumTextPage in your EDD to make it easier to import the format into your chapters.

Equation Elements

Exercise 3: Defining an Equation and Specifying Its InitialObjectFormat

In this exercise, you will:

- Redefine the Section element to contain optional EQ elements
- Define the EQ element as an Equation, using the InitialObjectFormat of LargeEquation

LargeEquation indicates the size of the characters in the equation, not the number of characters the equation can have. The user can specify a different equation size without incurring a format rule override.

1. In the EDD, locate the Section element definition.

2. In the Document Window, add EQ to the GeneralRule as follows:

```
Head, (((Para, (WarnNote | List | PartsTable | EQ)?)+, (Section,
Section+)?) | (Section, Section+))
```

[[**Element (Container):** Section]
    [[**General rule:** Head, (((Para, (WarnNote | List | PartsTable | EQ)?)+, (Section, Section+)?) | (Section, Section+))]
    [**Inclusions:** TextRange]

3. Insert another Element element and tag it EQ.

   a. In the Structure View, click below the last Element element.

   b. From the Element Catalog, insert an Element element.

      An Element element and a Tag child element appear.

   c. In the Tag element, type: EQ

4. Define EQ as an Equation.

   a. Click below the Tag element.

   b. From the Element Catalog, insert Equation.

      Equation element appears.

5. From the Element Catalog, insert InitialObjectFormat.

   InitialObjectFormat element appears.

6. Insert AllContextsRule.

   AllContextsRule element appears.

7. Insert LargeEquation.

   LargeEquation element appears.

8. Save your changes.

Exercise 4:   Reimporting and Testing the Equation Element

In this exercise, you will reimport the EDD into the structured template and test your element definitions for Section and EQ.

1. Reimport your element definitions and fix any errors.

    a. In testdoc.fm, from the File menu, choose Import > Element Definitions.

        Import Element Definitions dialog appears.

    b. From the Import from Document popup menu, choose EDD.fm.

    c. Click Import.

        An alert box appears indicating "Element definitions have been imported from the EDD"

    d. Click OK to close the alert box.

    e. If you had errors in the element definitions, edit your EDD and reimport.

2. In the Structure View, click in any Section element but below a Para element.

3. From the Element Catalog, insert an EQ element.

    An equation frame appears with the question mark (?) in the middle of the frame selected.

    [[item 2]]]
    [para text]]]

4. Save your changes.

Graphic Elements

Exercise 5:   Defining a Graphic and Specifying Its InitialObjectFormat

In this exercise, you will:

- Redefine the Section element to contain optional Figure elements
- Redefine the Item element to contain optional Figure elements
- Define the Figure element as a container of Caption followed by Graphic, with an AutoInsertion of Caption
- Define the Caption element as a Container of <TEXT>
- Define the Graphic element as a Graphic with an InitialObjectFormat of ImportedGraphic

ImportedGraphic indicates that the Import File dialog, rather than the Anchored Frame dialog, will open when the Graphic element is inserted. The user can close the Import File dialog and use the Anchored Frame dialog without incurring a format rule override.

1. In the EDD, locate the Section element definition.

2. In the Document Window, add Figure to the GeneralRule as follows:

```
Head, (((Para, (WarnNote | List | PartsTable | EQ | Figure)?)+,
(Section, Section+)?) | (Section, Section+))
```

> [[**Element (Container):** Section]
>   [[**General rule:** Head, (((Para, (WarnNote | List | PartsTable | EQ | Figure)?)+, (Section, Section+)?) |
>   (Section, Section+))]

3. In the EDD, locate the Item element definition.

4. In the Document Window, add Figure to the GeneralRule as follows:

```
(Para, (WarnNote | Figure)?)+
```

> [[**Element (Container):** Item]
>   [[**General rule:** (Para, (WarnNote | Figure)?)+]

5. Insert another Element element and tag it Figure.

    a. In the Structure View, click below the last Element element.

    b. From the Element Catalog, insert an Element element.

       An Element element and a Tag child element appear.

    c. In the Tag element, type: `Figure`

6. Define Figure as a Container of Caption, Graphic.

    a. Click below the Tag element.

    b. From the Element Catalog, insert Container.

       Container element and GeneralRule child element appear.

    c. In the GeneralRule element, type: `Caption, Graphic`

7. Define Figure as having an AutoInsertion of Caption.

    a. Click below the Figure's GeneralRule element.

    b. From the Element Catalog, insert AutoInsertions.

       AutoInsertions element with InsertChild element appear.

    c. In the InsertChild element, type: `Caption`

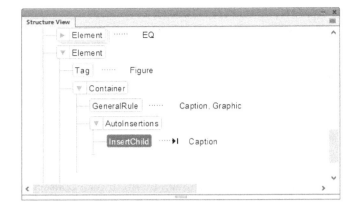

8. Insert another Element element and tag it Caption.

    a. In the Structure View, click below the last Element element.

    b. From the Element Catalog, insert an Element element.

       An Element element and a Tag child element appear.

    c. In the Tag element, type: `Caption`

9. Define Caption as a Container of <TEXT>

    a. Click below the Tag element.

    b. From the Element Catalog, insert Container.

       Container element and GeneralRule child element appear.

    c. In the GeneralRule element, type: `<TEXT>`

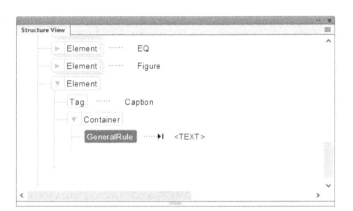

10. Insert another Element element and tag it Graphic.

    a. In the Structure View, click below the last Element element.

    b. From the Element Catalog, insert an Element element.

       An Element element and a Tag child element appear.

    c. In the Tag element, type: `Graphic`

11. Define Graphic as a Graphic.

    a. Click below the Tag element.

    b. From the Element Catalog, insert a Graphic element.

12. From the Element Catalog, insert InitialObjectFormat.

    InitialObjectFormat element appears.

13. Insert AllContextsRule.

    AllContextsRule element appears.

14. Insert ImportedGraphicFile.

    ImportedGraphicFile element appears.

15. Save your changes.

Exercise 6: Reimporting and Testing the Graphic Element

In this exercise, you will reimport the EDD into the structured template and test your element definitions for Section, Item, Figure, Caption, and Graphic.

1. Reimport your element definitions and fix any errors.

    a. In `testdoc.fm`, from the File menu, choose Import > Element Definitions.

       Import Element Definitions dialog appears.

    b. From the Import from Document popup menu, choose `EDD.fm`.

    c. Click Import.

       An alert box appears indicating "Element definitions have been imported from the EDD"

    d. Click OK to close the alert box.

    e. If you had errors in the element definitions, edit your EDD and reimport.

2. In the Structure View, click in any Section element but below a Para element.

3. From the Element Catalog, insert a Figure element.

    Figure element and Caption child element appear.

4. In the Caption element, type:
    `Caption for Figure`

5. Click below the Caption element, on the line descending from the Figure element.

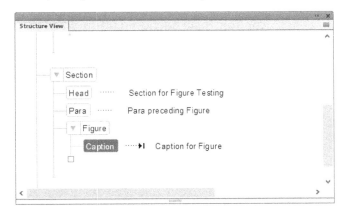

6. Insert a Graphic element.

    The Import dialog appears.

7. If necessary, change to your class files directory.

8. Select sidedoor.tif.

9. If necessary, select Import by Reference.

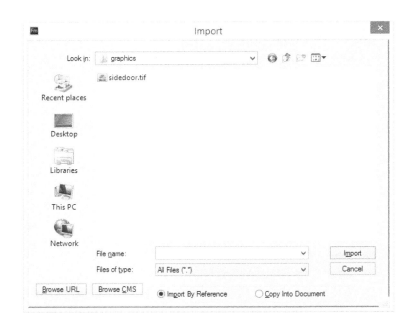

10. Click Import.

    The Imported Graphic Scaling dialog appears.

11. Select 150 dpi and click Set.

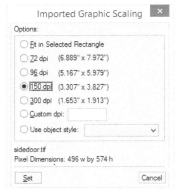

The sample graphic appears below the caption, in an anchored frame sized to fit the graphic.

12. Click in any Item element but below a Para element.

13. Insert a Figure element and test by adding caption and sidedoor.tif as above.

    A Figure element with child elements appears.

14. Save your changes.

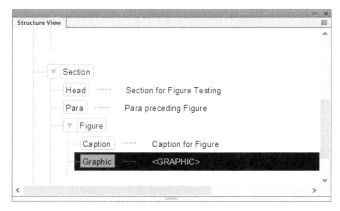

Marker Elements

Exercise 7:   Defining a Marker and Specifying Its InitialObjectFormat

In this exercise, you will:

- Redefine the Para element to contain optional IndexEntry elements
- Define the IndexEntry element as a Marker, using the InitialObjectFormat of Index

Index will be the preselected marker type in the Insert Marker dialog when the user inserts the IndexEntry elements. The user can select a different marker type without incurring a format rule override.

1. In the EDD, locate the Para element definition.

2. In the Document Window, change the GeneralRule as follows:

   [[**Element (Container):** Para]
      [[**General rule:** (<TEXT> | Footnote | XRef | IndexEntry)+]]]

   ```
   (<TEXT> | Footnote | XRef | IndexEntry)+
   ```

3. Insert another Element element and tag it IndexEntry.

   a. In the Structure View, click below the last Element element.

   b. From the Element Catalog, insert an Element element.

      An Element element and a Tag child element appear.

   c. In the Tag element, type: IndexEntry

4. Define IndexEntry as a Marker.

   a. Click below the Tag element.

   b. From the Element Catalog, insert Marker.

      Marker element appears.

5. From the Element Catalog, insert InitialObjectFormat.

   InitialObjectFormat element appears.

6. Insert AllContextsRule.

   AllContextsRule element appears.

7. Insert MarkerType.

   MarkerType element appears.

8. Insert Index.

   Index element appears.

9. Save your changes.

Exercise 8:   Reimporting and Testing the Marker Element

In this exercise, you will reimport the EDD into the structured template and test your element definitions for Para and IndexEntry.

1. Reimport your element definitions and fix any errors.

   a. In `testdoc.fm`, from the File menu, choose Import > Element Definitions.

      Import Element Definitions dialog appears.

   b. From the Import from Document popup menu, choose `EDD.fm`.

   c. Click Import.

      An alert box appears indicating "Element definitions have been imported from the EDD"

   d. Click OK to close the alert box.

   e. If you had errors in the element definitions, edit your EDD and reimport.

2. In the Structure View, click in any Para element.

3. From the Element Catalog, insert an IndexEntry element.

   The Insert Marker dialog appears with Index preselected from the Marker Type popup menu.

4. In the Marker Text dialog, type: `Sample index entry`

5. Click New Marker.

   In the Structure View, the IndexEntry element appears with "Sample index entry" to the right of the element bubble. Also, if you view your text symbols (View > Text Symbols) you will see a marker symbol (**T**) at the insertion point in the Document Window.

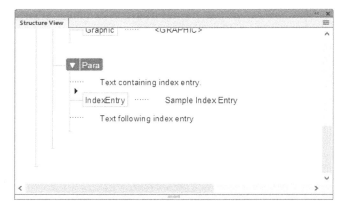

6. Save your changes.

SystemVariableFormatRule

Required part of element definition for SystemVariable elements only

- Identifies which system variable to use
- SystemVariableFormatRule is not only a suggestion—user cannot change to another format without creating format override

You can specify a SystemVariableFormatRule with:

- AllContextsRule—wherever the element appears
- ContextRule—when element is in certain context
- LevelRule—when element is nested a specified number of levels in a specified ancestor
- DefaultSystemVariable—uses FilenameLong system variable

Exercise 9:   Defining a System Variable and Specifying Its Format Rule

In this exercise, you will:

- Redefine the Para element to contain a Date element
- Define the Date element as a System Variable, using the SystemVariableFormatRule of CurrentDateLong.

The Current Date (Long) system variable will be inserted when the user inserts the Data elements. The user *cannot* select a different system variable without incurring a format rule override.

1. In the EDD, locate the Para element definition.

2. In the Document Window, add **Date** to the GeneralRule as follows:

   [[**Element (Container):** Para]
   [[**General rule:** (<TEXT> | Footnote | XRef | IndexEntry | Date)+]]]

   ```
   (<TEXT> | Footnote | XRef | IndexEntry | Date)+
   ```

3. Insert another Element element and tag it Date.

   a. In the Structure View, click below the last Element element.

   b. From the Element Catalog, insert an Element element.

   An Element element and a Tag child element appear.

   c. In the Tag element, type: Date

4. Define Date as a SystemVariable.

   a. Click below the Tag element.

   b. From the Element Catalog, insert SystemVariable.

   The SystemVariable element appears.

5. From the Element Catalog, insert SystemVariableFormatRule.

   The SystemVariableFormatRule element appears.

6. Insert AllContextsRule.

   AllContextsRule element appears.

7. Insert UseSystemVariable.

   UseSystemVariable element appears.

8. Insert CurrentDateLong.

   CurrentDateLong element appears.

9. Save your changes.

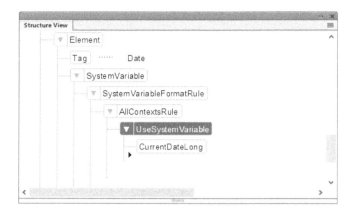

Exercise 10: Reimporting and Testing the System Variable Element

In this exercise, you will reimport the EDD into the structured template and test your element definitions for Para and Date.

1. Reimport your element definitions and fix any errors.

   a. In `testdoc.fm`, from the File menu, choose Import > Element Definitions.

      Import Element Definitions dialog appears.

   b. From the Import from Document popup menu, choose `EDD.fm`.

   c. Click Import.

      An alert box appears indicating "Element definitions have been imported from the EDD"

   d. Click OK to close the alert box.

   e. If you had errors in the element definitions, edit your EDD and reimport.

2. In the Structure View, click in any Para element.

3. From the Element Catalog, insert a Date element.

   Today's date appears at the insertion point.

4. Save your changes.

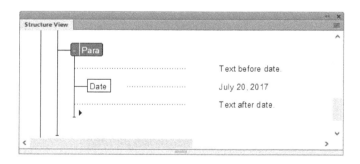

Chapter 9: Attribute List

Introduction

This chapter focuses on defining attributes for elements in the element's AttributeList.

Objectives

- Review uses of attributes
- Review basic types of attributes and their parts
- Specify the attribute Name
- Specify the attribute Type
- Indicate whether the attribute is Optional or Required
- Indicate whether the attribute is ReadOnly
- For attribute of numeric type (Integer, Integers, Real, Reals), define a Range of values
- For attributes of type Choice, define a list of Choices
- For attributes indicated as Optional, specify a Default

Overview

Optional part of all element definitions

- Refers to one or more attributes
- Used for general descriptions, cross-referencing, formatting, and prefixing

Potential attributes for general descriptions:

- Class attribute of Report element identifies security
- Version attribute of Chapter element identifies revision
- Author attribute of Section element identifies writer

Attributes used for cross-referencing elements:

- Define UniqueID type attribute for any element (Container, Object, Table, Table Part) that might be cross-referenced (Figure, Table, Title, Head)

  User can enter meaningful unique identification for element

- Define UniqueID type attribute as ReadOnly if you don't want user to enter or edit the value

  If referenced, FrameMaker will generate a value

- If ReadOnly, define UniqueID type attribute as Optional to prevent "missing attribute value" validation error if element never referenced
- Define IDReference type attribute for any cross-reference type element (XRef, TableXRef, FigXRef) used to refer to other elements
- Define IDReference type attribute as Required to force a link to a UniqueID attribute value for validity

- Define **IDReference** type attribute as **ReadOnly** if you don't want user to enter or edit the value
- If referenced element has no **UniqueID** value, FrameMaker generates one and then copies generated **UniqueID** for **IDReference** attribute value

Attributes used for formatting elements:

Name/value attribute pairs in format rule can drive formatting of:
- Initial table format
- Initial object format
- System variable format
- Paragraph formatting
- Text-range formatting

Attributes used for prefixing elements:

Format rules can use attribute values to provide text for prefix or suffix:
- **Prefix** is text range that appears at beginning of element (before element's content)
- **Suffix** is text range that appears at end of element (after content)

Basic Types of Attributes and Their Parts

Defaults can only be provided for attribute values defined as Optional (not Required). Plural attribute types (Strings, Integers, Reals) may have more than one default value

Attribute Name

- Required part of all attribute definitions
- Type descriptive name of attribute
- Up to 255 characters, but better to keep concise
- Case-sensitive
- Cannot contain white space
- Cannot contain any of these special characters:
  - ( ) & | , * + ? < > % [ ] = ! ; : { } "

Attribute Type

- Required part of all attribute definitions
- Select one of predefined attribute types

Optional or Required

- Required part of all attribute definitions
- Specify whether or not attribute requires value for each instance of element
- If attribute requires but does not have value, FrameMaker identifies attribute as invalid

ReadOnly

- Optional part of all attribute definitions
- Specify whether to restrict users from entering and editing attribute value

Range

- Optional part of attribute definitions for numeric types:

  Integer, Integers, Real, Reals

- Specify whether to restrict users to an inclusive range of values

  Attributes window displays range of values when this attribute is selected

Choices

- Required part of attribute definitions for **Choice** attributes
- Type list of possible choices
- **Attributes** window displays choices in **Choices** popup menu when this attribute is selected
- **Choices:**
  - Up to 255 characters
  - Can have white-space characters
  - Cannot have any of these special characters:

    ( ) & | , * + ? < > % [ ] = ! ; : { } "

Default

- Optional part of attribute definitions for:

  String or **Strings**, **Integer** or **Integers**, **Real** or **Reals**, **Choice**

  But only if defined as **Optional** attribute value (not **Required**)

- Type default value to use if user elects not to enter a value
- Can specify more than one default value for plural types (**Strings**, **Integers**, **Reals**)

Defining Attributes for General Descriptions

Exercise 1:   Defining a Required String Attribute

In this exercise, you will define a **Required String** attribute named **Author** for the **Chapter** element by:

- Inserting an **AttributeList** element and typing the **Name** as **Author**
- Inserting a **String** element to specify **Author's** attribute type
- Inserting a **Required** element to indicate that a value is required

To do this:

1. If it is not already open, from your class files directory, open EDD.fm, the EDD you've been modifying throughout the class.

If you did not finish the previous chapter's modifications to the EDD, please open **Chapter 9-start Attributes.fm** instead, and save it in your class files directory as EDD.fm.

If needed, download the class files by visiting http://www.techcommtools.com/struct-auth-files/

2. In the EDD, locate the **Chapter** element definition.

3. Click below the **Chapter's GeneralRule** element (or click below the **ValidHighestLevel** element if you inserted it below, rather than above, the **Chapter's GeneralRule**).

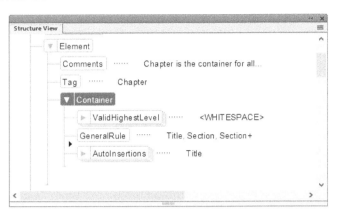

4. From the **Element Catalog**, insert **AttributeList**.

   An **Attribute** child element inserted automatically with a nested **Name** child element.

5. In the **Name** element, type: Author

6. Click below the **Name** element, on line descending from Attribute element.

7. From the **Element Catalog**, insert **String**.

   A **String** element appears with insertion point below it.

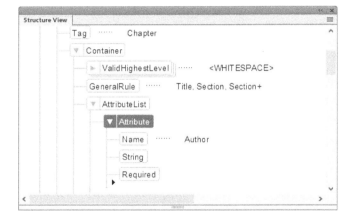

8. From the **Element Catalog**, insert **Required**.

   A **Required** element appears.

9. Save your changes.

Exercise 2:   Defining an Optional Real Attribute with a Range and Default

In this exercise, you will define an **Optional Real** attribute named **Version**, including a **Range** limitation and a **Default** value, for the **Chapter** element, by:

- Inserting an **AttributeList** element and typing the **Name** as **Version**
- Inserting a **Real** element to specify **Version's** attribute type
- Inserting an **Optional** element to indicate that a value is optional
- Inserting a **Range** element and typing the allowed range
- Inserting a **Default** element and typing the
- default value

1. In the EDD, locate the **Chapter** element definition.

2. In the **Structure View**, click below the **Author** attribute element, on the line descending from the **AttributeList** element.

3. From the **Element Catalog**, insert **Attribute**.

    A **Name** child element inserted automatically.

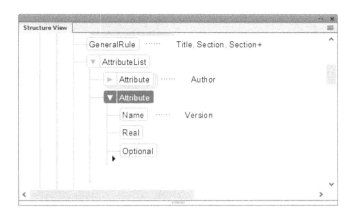

4. In the **Name** element, type: `Version`

5. Click below the **Name** element, on line descending from the **Attribute** element.

6. From the **Element Catalog**, insert a **Real** element.

    A **Real** element appears with insertion point below it.

7. From the **Element Catalog**, insert **Optional**.

    An **Optional** element appears with insertion point below it.

8. From the **Element Catalog**, insert **Range**.

    A **Range** element and **From** child element appear.

9. In **From** element, type: `1`

10. Click below the **From** element, on line descending from **Range** element.

11. From the **Element Catalog**, insert **To**.

    A **To** element appears.

12. In the **To** element, type: `5`

13. Click below the **Range** element, on line descending from the **Attribute** element.

14. From the **Element Catalog**, insert **Default**.

    The **Default** element appears.

15. In the **Default** element, type: `1`

16. Save your changes.

Exercise 3: Reimporting and Testing Attributes

In this exercise, you will reimport the EDD into the structured template, verify that **Always Prompt for Attribute Values** is turned on, and test your attributes on **Chapter**.

1. Reimport your element definitions and fix any errors.

   a. In `testdoc.fm`, from the **File** menu, choose **Import > Element Definitions**.

      The **Import Element Definitions** dialog appears.

   b. From **Import from Document** popup menu, choose `EDD.fm`.

   c. Click **Import**.

      An alert box appears indicating "**Element definitions have been imported from the EDD**"

   d. Click **OK** to close the alert box.

   e. If you had errors in the element definitions, edit your EDD and reimport.

2. Verify that **Always Prompt for Attribute Values** is turned on.

   The author can choose to be prompted for attribute values upon insertion of elements.

   a. From the **Element** menu, choose **New Element Options**.

      The **New Element Options** dialog appears.

   b. If not already on, turn on **Always Prompt for Attribute Values**.

   c. Click **Set**.

3. In the **Structure View**, select and delete the **Chapter** element.

   Since **Chapter** is the highest-level element, all the contents disappear.

4. From the **Element Catalog**, insert a **Chapter** element.

   The **Attributes for New Element** dialog appears.

5. In the **Attribute Name** scroll list, select **Author**.

6. Type a string value for the **Author** attribute and click **Set Value**.

7. In the **Attribute Name** scroll list, select **Version**.

   The dialog displays the properties of the **Version** attribute.

8. Type a number that is not between `1.0` and `5.0` and click **Set Value**.

   An alert appears, indicating your value is invalid.

9. Click **OK** to dismiss the alert.

10. Click **Insert Element**.

    The **Version** uses the default value of **1.0**.

11. Save your changes.

Defining Attributes for Prefixes and Formatting

Exercise 4:   Defining an optional choice attribute to provide a prefix

In this exercise, you will define an optional choice attribute named **MessageType**, including available choices and a **Default** value, for the **WarnNote** element, by:

- Inserting an **AttributeList** element and typing the **Name** as **MessageType**
- Inserting a **Choice** element to specify **MessageType** attribute type
- Inserting an **Optional** element to indicate that a value is optional
- Inserting a **Choices** element and typing the values to appear in the **Choices** popup menu
- Inserting a **Default** element and typing the default value

In a later exercise, you will use the value of the **MessageType** attribute to control the prefix of the **WarnNote** element.

1. In the EDD, locate the **WarnNote** element definition.

2. In the **Structure View**, click below **WarnNote's GeneralRule** element.

3. From the **Element Catalog**, insert **AttributeList**.

    An **Attribute** child element inserted automatically with nested **Name** child element.

4. In the **Name** element, type: `MessageType`

5. Click below the **Name** element, on line descending from **Attribute** element.

6. From the **Element Catalog**, insert **Choice**.

    A **Choice** element appears with insertion point below it.

7. From the **Element Catalog**, insert **Optional**.

    An **Optional** element appears with insertion point below it.

8. From the **Element Catalog**, insert **Choices**.

    A **Choices** element appears.

9. In the **Choices** element, type:
    `NOTE, WARNING`

10. Click below the **Choices** element, on the line descending from the **Attribute** element.

11. From the **Element Catalog**, insert **Default**.

    A **Default** element appears.

12. In the **Default** element, type: `NOTE`

13. Save your changes.

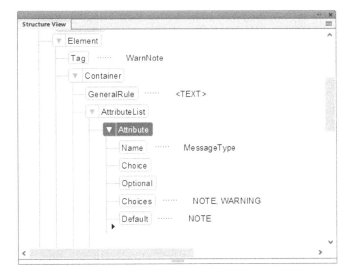

14. Reimport your element definitions and fix any errors.

    a. In `testdoc.fm`, from the **File** menu, choose **Import > Element Definitions**.

       The **Import Element Definitions** dialog appears.

    b. From **Import from Document** popup menu, choose `EDD.fm`.

    c. Click **Import**.

       An alert box appears indicating "**Element definitions have been imported from the EDD**"

    d. Click **OK** to close the alert box.

    e. If you had errors in the element definitions, edit your EDD and reimport.

15. From the **Element Catalog**, insert **Section**, **Head**, **Para**, and **WarnNote** elements.

    The **Attributes for New Element** dialog appears with the **WarnNote** element.

16. In the **Attribute Name** scroll list, select **MessageType**.

    The dialog displays the properties of the **MessageType** attribute.

17. From the attribute value **Choices** popup menu, select **WARNING** and click **Insert Element**.

18. Click **Insert Element**.

    The **Structure View** displays the **WARNING** attribute value. Later you will use this attribute to provide a prefix for your content.

19. Save your changes.

Exercise 5: Defining an Optional Choice Attribute to Provide Formatting

In this exercise, you will define an **Optional Choice** attribute named **ListType**, including available choices and a **Default** value, for the **List** element, by:

- Inserting an **AttributeList** element and typing the **Name** as **ListType**
- Inserting a **Choice** element to specify **ListType**'s attribute type
- Inserting an **Optional** element to indicate that a value is optional
- Inserting a **Choices** element and typing the values to appear in the **Choices** popup menu
- Inserting a **Default** element and typing the default value

In a later exercise, you will use the value of the **ListType** attribute to control the formatting of the children of the **List** element.

1. In the EDD, locate the **List** element definition.

2. In the **Structure View**, click below the **List**'s **GeneralRule** element.

3. From the **Element Catalog**, insert an **AttributeList**.

   An **Attribute** child element is inserted, along with an automatically nested **Name** child element.

4. In the **Name** element, type: `ListType`

5. Click below the **Name** element, on line descending from **Attribute** element.

6. Insert **Choice**.

   A **Choice** element appears with insertion point below it.

7. Insert **Optional**.

   An **Optional** element appears with insertion point below it.

8. Insert **Choices**.

   A **Choices** element appears.

9. In the **Choices** element, type:
   `Bulleted, Numbered`

10. Click below **Choices** element, on line descending from **Attribute** element.

11. Insert **Default**.

    A **Default** element appears.

12. In the Default element, type:
    `Bulleted`

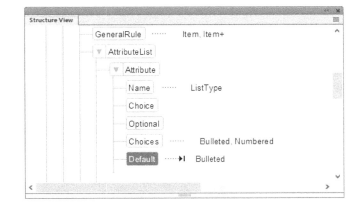

13. Save your changes.

14. Reimport your element definitions and fix any errors.

    a. In `testdoc.fm`, from the File menu, choose **Import > Element Definitions**.

       The **Import Element Definitions** dialog appears.

    b. From the **Import from Document** popup menu, choose `EDD.fm`.

    c. Click **Import**.

       An alert box appears indicating "**Element definitions have been imported from the EDD**"

    d. Click **OK** to close the alert box.

    e. If you had errors in the element definitions, edit your EDD and reimport.

15. From the **Element Catalog**, insert another **Para** element, and below it insert a **List** element.

    The **Attributes for New Element** dialog appears.

16. In the **Attribute Name** scroll list, select **ListType**.
17. From the attribute value **Choices** popup menu, select **Numbered** and click **Set Value**.

    You will set numbering for this list in another lesson.

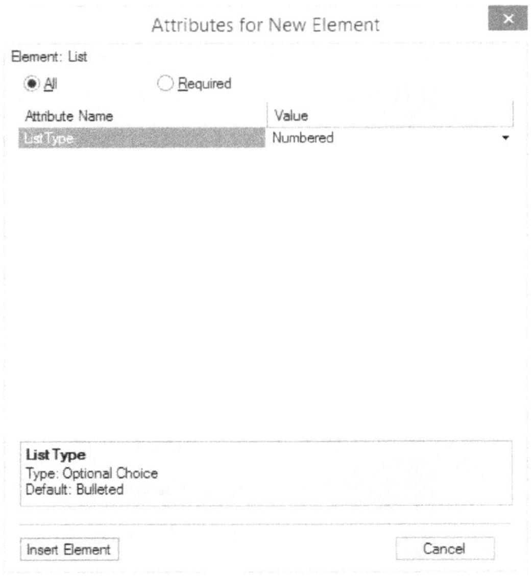

18. Click **Insert Element**.

    The **Structure View** displays the attribute value.

19. Save your changes.

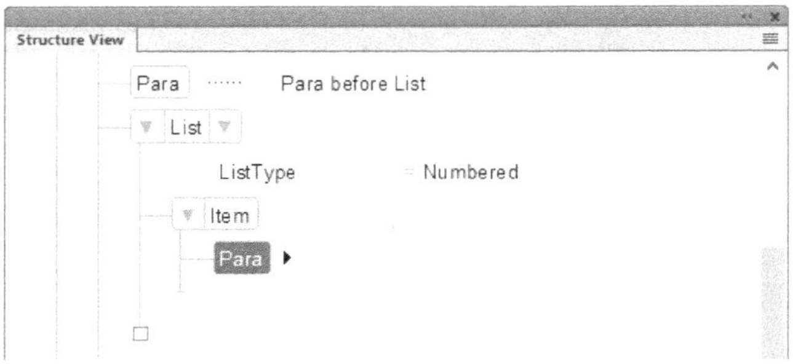

Exercise 6: Defining an optional choice attribute to provide InitialObjectFormat

In this exercise, you will define an optional choice attribute named **ReadyToImport**, including available choices and a Default value, for the Figure element, by:

- Inserting an **AttributeList** element and typing the Name as **ReadyToImport**
- Inserting a **Choice** element to specify **ReadyToImport**'s attribute type
- Inserting an **Optional** element to indicate that a value is optional
- Inserting a **Choices** element and typing the values to appear in the **Choices** popup menu
- Inserting a **Default** element and typing the default value

In a later exercise, you will use the value of the **ReadyToImport** attribute to control the appearance of the **Import File** dialog or **Anchored Frame** dialog when inserting the **Figure** element's child **Graphic** element.

1. In the EDD, locate the **Figure** element definition.
2. In the **Structure View**, click below **Figure**'s **GeneralRule** element.
3. From the **Element Catalog**, insert **AttributeList**.

   An **Attribute** child element inserted automatically with nested **Name** child element.

4. In the Name element, type: **ReadyToImport**

5. Click below the **Name** element, on line descending from **Attribute** element.

6. Insert **Choice**.

   A **Choice** element appears with insertion point below it.

7. Insert **Optional**.

   An Optional element appears with insertion point below it.

8. Insert **Choices**.

   A **Choices** element appears.

9. In the **Choices** element, type: Yes, No

10. Click below **Choices** element, on line descending from **Attribute** element.

11. Insert **Default**.

    A **Default** element appears.

12. In the **Default** element, type: No

13. Save your changes.

14. Reimport your element definitions and fix any errors.

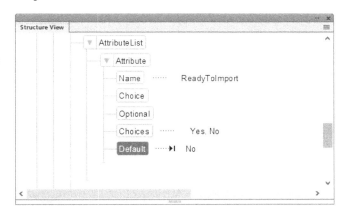

   a. In testdoc.fm, from the **File** menu, choose **Import > Element Definitions**.

      The **Import Element Definitions** dialog appears.

   b. From the **Import from Document** popup menu, choose EDD.fm.

   c. Click **Import**.

      An alert box appears indicating "**Element definitions have been imported from the EDD**"

   d. Click **OK** to close the alert box.

   e. If you had errors in the element definitions, edit your EDD and reimport.

15. From the **Element Catalog**, insert a **Figure** element.

    The **Attributes for New Element** dialog appears.

16. In the **Attribute Name** scroll list, select **ReadyToImport** .

    The dialog displays the properties of the **ReadyToImport** attribute.

17. From the attribute value **Choices** popup menu, select **Yes** and click **Set Value**.

18. Click **Insert Element**.

    The **Structure View** displays the **ReadyToImport** attribute value.

19. Save your changes.

Defining Attributes for Cross-Referencing

Exercise 7:   Defining an Optional, ReadOnly **UniqueID** Attribute for a Source

In this exercise, you will set up an **Optional UniqueID** for cross-referencing by creating an attribute named **ID**, including a **ReadOnly** specification, for the **Title**, **Head**, **PartsTable**, and **Figure** elements, by:

- Inserting an **AttributeList** element and typing the **Name** as **ID**
- Inserting a **UniqueID** element to specify the attribute type for **ID**
- Inserting an **Optional** element to indicate that a value is optional
- Inserting a **SpecialAttributeControls** element containing a **ReadOnly** element to prevent the user from editing the value

In a later exercise, you will use the value of the **ID** for cross-referencing.

1. In the EDD, locate the **Title** element definition.

2. In the **Structure View**, click below **GeneralRule** for **Title**.

3. From the **Element Catalog**, insert **AttributeList**.

    An **Attribute** child element inserted automatically with a nested child element.

4. In the **Name** element, type: `ID`

5. Click below the **Name** element, on line descending from **Attribute** element.

6. Insert **UniqueID**.

    A **UniqueID** element appears with insertion point below it.

7. Insert **Optional**.

    An **Optional** element appears with insertion point below it.

8. Insert a **Special Attribute Controls** element below **Optional**.

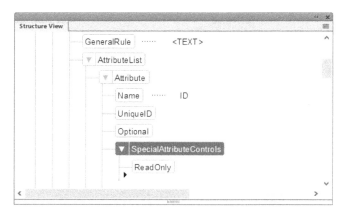

9. Insert a ReadOnly element as a child of **SpecialAttributeControls**

    A **ReadOnly** element appears.

10. Save your changes.

11. Repeat for the **Head** element.

    a. In the EDD, locate the **Head** element definition.

    b. In the **Structure View**, click below the **Exclusion** element in the **Head** element definition.

    c. From the **Element Catalog**, insert **AttributeList**.

    First Attribute child element inserted automatically with nested **Name** child element.

    d. In the **Name** element, type: ID

    e. Click below the **Name** element, on line descending from **Attribute** element.

    f. Insert **UniqueID**.

    A **UniqueID** element appears with insertion point below it.

    g. Insert **Optional**.

    An **Optional** element appears with insertion point below it.

    h. Insert **ReadOnly**.

    A **ReadOnly** element appears.

    i. Save your changes.

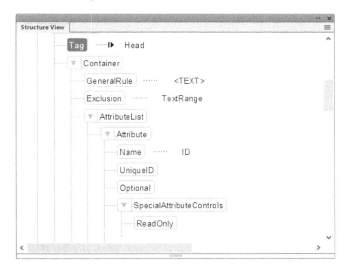

 You can use Copy/Paste to speed entry of common attribute lists and individual attributes.

12. Repeat for the **PartsTable** element.

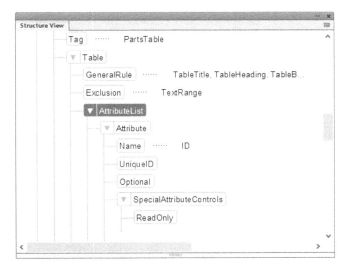

13. Repeat for the **Figure** element.

    Since already has an **AttributeList** element, you will add an additional **Attribute** element as a child to the existing **AttributeList** element.

14. Save your changes.

15. Reimport your element definitions and fix any errors.

    a. In testdoc.fm, from the File menu, choose **Import > Element Definitions**.

       The **Import Element Definitions** dialog appears.

    b. From **Import from Document** popup menu, choose EDD.fm.

    c. Click **Import**.

       An alert box appears indicating "**Element definitions have been imported from the EDD**"

    d. Click **OK** to close the alert box.

    e. If you had errors in the element definitions, edit your EDD and reimport.

16. From the **Element Catalog**, insert one each of **Title, Head, PartsTable** and **Figure** elements.

    Each new element entered has the **ID** attribute, which will populate when cross-referenced.

17. Save your changes.

![computer icon] **Exercise 8:   Defining a Required, ReadOnly IDReference attribute for XRef**

In this exercise, you will define an **Required, IDReference** attribute named **IDRef**, including a **ReadOnly** specification, for the **XRef** element, by:

- Inserting an **AttributeList** element and typing the **Name** as **IDRef**
- Inserting an **IDReference** element to specify the **IDRef** attribute type
- Inserting an **Required** element to indicate that a value is required
- Inserting a **ReadOnly** element to prevent the user from editing the value

1. In the EDD, locate the **XRef** element definition.

2. In the **Structure View**, click above **XRef's InitialObjectFormat** element.

3. From the **Element Catalog**, insert **AttributeList**.

The **Attribute** child element inserted automatically with a nested **Name** child element.

4. In the **Name** element, type: `IDRef`

5. Click below the **Name** element, on line descending from **Attribute** element.

6. Insert **IDReference**.

IDReference element appears with insertion point below it.

7. Insert **Required**.

A **Required** element appears with insertion point below it.

8. Insert **ReadOnly**.

ReadOnly element appears.

9. Save your changes.

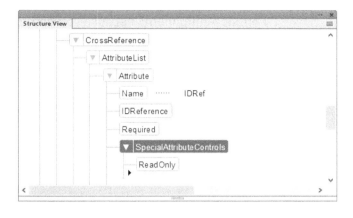

10. Reimport your element definitions and fix any errors.

a. In `testdoc.fm`, from the File menu, choose **Import > Element Definitions**.

The **Import Element Definitions** dialog appears.

b. From **Import from Document** popup menu, choose `EDD.fm`.

c. Click **Import**.

An alert box appears indicating "**Element definitions have been imported from the EDD**"

d. Click **OK** to close the alert box.

e. If you had errors in the element definitions, edit your EDD and reimport.

11. From the **Element Catalog**, insert an **XRef** element.

The **Cross-Reference** dialog appears.

12. From the **Source Type** popup menu, choose **Elements Listed in Order**.

The **Source Type** scroll list displays all element tags with an attribute of type UniqueID:

- Figure
- Head
- PartsTable
- Title

13. From the **Source Type** scroll list, select **Head**.

The **Source Text** scroll list displays all occurrences of the **Head** element in the document.

14. In the **Source Text** scroll list, select any one of your **Head** elements.

    ElemNumTextPage is already chosen from the **Format** popup menu, because you defined it as the **InitialObjectFormat** for **XRef**.

15. Click **Insert**.

    [Para containing xref.[See Another Section Heading, on page 1.]]]
    [[Another Section Heading]]]

    The cross-reference appears. FrameMaker supplies the value for the **ReadOnly UniqueID** type attribute named **ID** on the cross-referenced **Head** element. FrameMaker pulls that value and enters it as the **ReadOnly IDReference** type attribute named **IDRef** on the **XRef** element.

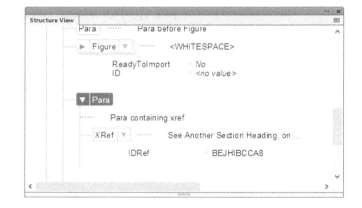

    Before inserting the **XRef** element, the **Section Head** had no **IDRef**. After inserting the **XRef**, the **Head ID** and corresponding **XRef IDRef** attributes have matching values.

16. Using the previous steps, insert **XRef** elements to **Title**, **PartsTable** and **Figure** elements.

 Note: You need to insert an element of a given type in your document before you can insert a cross-reference to that type of element.

17. Save your changes.

Chapter 10: AllContext formatting rules

Introduction

This chapter focuses on writing the **TextFormatRules** for **Container**, **Footnote**, **Table** and table part elements.

Objectives

- Define parts of text format rules
- Specify an **ElementPgfFormatTag**
- Write an:
    - AllContextsRule
    - **ContextRule** with **If**, **ElseIf**, **Else** clauses
    - **LevelRule** with **If**, **ElseIf**, **Else** clauses
- Refer to:
    - **ParagraphFormatTag/CharacterFormatTag**
    - Individual paragraph/text-range properties
    - **FormatChangeListTag**
- Analyze syntax for naming ancestors, siblings and attribute values
- Define subRules and multiple rules
- Write a **ContextLabel**
- Define a **FormatChangeList/FormatChangeListLimits**

Overview

Optional part of element definitions for:

- Container
- Table, TableTitle, TableHeading, TableBody, TableFooting, TableRow, TableCell
- Footnote

Identifies formatting for text in element:

- Rules for **Table**, **TableHeading**, **TableBody**, **TableFooting**, **TableRow** specify formatting only for text in descendant **TableTitle** and **TableCell** elements
- Changes are considered overrides
- When user reimports element definitions, user can keep or remove overrides

The parts that make up TextFormatRules

Part	Description
ElementPgfFormatTag	• Optional, zero or one, before other parts • "Named" base paragraph format stored in document • Defines all aspects of text and paragraph formatting—basic, default font, pagination, numbering, advanced, table cell
AllContextsRule	• Optional, zero or more, in any order • Formatting change wherever the element appears
ContextRule	• Optional, zero or more, in any order • With separate clauses: If—one ElseIf—zero or more Else—zero or one • Formatting change when element is in certain context
LevelRule	• Optional, zero or more, in any order • With separate clauses: If—one ElseIf—zero or more Else—zero or one • Formatting change when element is nested a specified number of levels in an ancestor

Each AllContextsRule, and If/ElseIf/Else clause in ContextRule and LevelRule can refer to:

• A named ParagraphFormatTag or CharacterFormatTag
• Individual formatting properties
• A FormatChangeList

Text formatting is hierarchical:

• An element can inherit properties from ancestors
• An element can pass on properties to descendants

First, FrameMaker determines which base paragraph format to apply:

• If element's definition specifies base paragraph format, that format is used
• If not, FrameMaker searches up through ancestors until it finds element with format and uses that format
• If reaches top of element's hierarchy without finding a format, uses default Body paragraph format

Second, determines formatting changes to apply:

- Goes back down through hierarchy to current element, cumulatively picking up formatting changes
- Changes can specify either:
    - Absolute values (fixed value, such as indent expressed as distance from left margin)
    - Relative values (change to current setting, such as amount to move indent)

If the current element is in a table:

- Formatting will not search beyond an ancestor **Table** element
- If no ancestors prior to **Table** element specify paragraph format, the paragraph format stored in the table format will be used

For text in a footnote element:

- No cascade beyond ancestor **Footnote** element
- If no paragraph formatting is specified within **Footnote** element, main flow footnotes will use the document's current footnote paragraph format and table footnotes will use the current table footnote paragraph format

If document is part of book:

- If FrameMaker does not find paragraph format in document (when searching outside **Table** or **Footnote**) FrameMaker will continue looking for a paragraph format in ancestor elements of book files
- If found in book hierarchy, FrameMaker uses that paragraph format
- If FrameMaker reaches top of book without finding paragraph format FrameMaker uses the default **Body** paragraph format stored in document
- When using paragraph format from hierarchy in book, FrameMaker goes back down through hierarchy to current element, cumulatively picking up formatting changes

Specifying the ElementPgfFormatTag

Reference to "named" base paragraph format stored in document

- Defines all properties of text and paragraph formatting—basic, default font, pagination, numbering, advanced, table cell
- If instance of element contains text, text's format is paragraph format plus any changes specified for current context in element's format rules
- Paragraph format is also passed on to element's descendants—until descendant provides different format
- Rules for **Table**, **TableHeading**, **TableBody**, **TableFooting**, **TableRow** specify formatting only for text in descendant **TableTitle** and **TableCell** elements

Exercise 1:   Specifying a Base Tag for the Entire Flow

In this exercise, you will specify an **ElementPgfFormatTag** of **Body** for the **Chapter** element, by inserting:

- **TextFormatRules** element
- **ElementPgfFormatTag** element and typing the **Tag** as **Body**

The paragraph tag **Body** will be inherited by all elements in the entire structure, unless another element specifies its own paragraph tag. Any individual format changes (such as a weight of bold or size of 14 points) defined in **Chapter** or its descendants will make changes to the properties defined in and inherited from the **Body** paragraph tag.

1. If it is not already open, from your class files directory, open EDD.fm, the EDD you'll be modifying throughout the class.

   If you did not finish the previous chapter's modifications to the EDD, please open **Chapter 10-start Formatting.fm** instead, and save it in your class files directory as EDD.fm.

If needed, download the class files by visiting http://www.techcommtools.com/struct-auth-files/

2. In the EDD, locate the **Chapter** element definition.

3. In the **Structure View**, click below **AutoInsertions** for the **Chapter** element.

4. From the **Element Catalog**, insert **TextFormatRules**.

   A **TextFormatRules** element appears.

5. Insert an **ElementPgfFormatTag**.

   An **ElementPgfFormatTag** element appears.

6. In **ElementPgfFormatTag** element, type: Body

7. Save your changes.

8. IMPORT AND TEST.

   All elements now explicitly use the **Body** paragraph format.

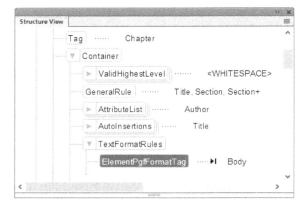

Writing an AllContextsRule

Specifies format that applies to element in all contexts in which it can occur, referring to:

- Named **ParagraphFormatTag** or **CharacterFormatTag** (if text range) stored in document
- Individual paragraph or text-range formatting properties
- Or **FormatChangeList**

Referring to Individual Formatting Properties

Format rule clauses can describe changes to any property in:

- **Paragraph Designer**, except **Next Paragraph Tag,** which is not used in structured documents
- **Character Designer**

PropertiesBasic	Set indentation, line spacing, paragraph alignment, paragraph spacing, and tab stops
PropertiesFont	Set font, size, and style of text in element
PropertiesPagination	Define placement of paragraph on page and determine how to break paragraph across columns and pages
PropertiesNumbering	Specify syntax and format for automatically generated string, such as number that appears at beginning of procedure step
PropertiesAdvanced	Set hyphenation and word spacing options and determine whether to display graphic with paragraph
PropertiesTableCell	Customize margins of cells and vertical alignment of text in them

With some properties, you type values, while other allow insertion of keyword child element (such as **Bold** or **Yes**)

With some numeric values, you can type either:

- Relative values (positive or negative)—added to current value to set new value
- Absolute values—overrides current value for property

Use a FormatChangeList to:

- Describe set of changes to format properties
- Prevent repeat typing of same changes used throughout EDD

Refer to a FormatChangeList by name in:

- Text format rules—**AllContextsRule, ContextRule, LevelRule**
- **PrefixRules** or **SuffixRules**
- **FirstParagraphRules** or **LastParagraphRules**

Exercise 2:   Specifying an AllContextsRule Referring to "Basic" Properties

In this exercise, you will specify an AllContextsRule for the Chapter element, that specifies the space above and below the element, by inserting:

- AllContextsRule element
- ParagraphFormatting element
- PropertiesBasic element
- ParagraphSpacing element
- SpaceAbove element and typing the space as 10 pt
- SpaceBelow element and typing the space as 10 pt

These changes to Chapter will be inherited by all elements in the entire structure, unless changed by another element's formatting.

1. In the EDD, locate the Chapter element definition.

2. In the Structure View, click below the ElementPgfFormatTag of the Chapter element, on the line descending from TextFormatRules.

3. From the Element Catalog, insert AllContextsRule.

    An AllContextsRule element appears.

4. To specify paragraph formatting, rather than text-range formatting, insert ParagraphFormatting.

    A ParagraphFormatting element appears.

5. Insert PropertiesBasic.

    A PropertiesBasic element appears.

6. Insert ParagraphSpacing.

7. Insert SpaceAbove and type: `10 pt`

8. Click below SpaceAbove element, on line descending from ParagraphSpacing element.

9. Insert SpaceBelow and type: `10 pt`

10. Save your changes.

11. IMPORT AND TEST.

    All elements have 10 points of space above and 10 points of space below.

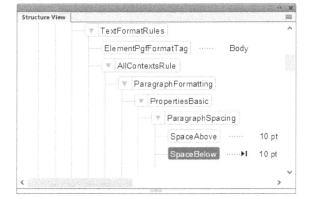

Exercise 3:   Specifying an AllContextsRule Referring to Many Properties

In this exercise, you will specify an **AllContextsRule** for the **Title** element that:

Changes the space below to an absolute value of 50 points using the following:

- **TextFormatRules** element
- **AllContextsRule** element
- **ParagraphFormatting** element
- **PropertiesBasic** element
- **ParagraphSpacing** element
- **SpaceBelow** element and typing the space as `50 pt`

Makes the text italic and 20 points:

- **PropertiesFont** element
- **Angle** element
- **Size** element and typing the size as `20 pt`

Adds an autonumber of `<$chapnum>.` followed by a space:

- **PropertiesNumbering** element
- **AutonumberFormat** element and typing `C:Chapter <$chapnum>.` and a space

Adds a reference frame called **Double Line**:

- **PropertiesAdvanced** element
- **FrameBelow** element and typing the name of the reference frame

To specify this rule, do this:

1. In the EDD, locate the **Title** element definition.
2. In the **Structure View**, click below the **AttributeList** of the **Title** element.
3. From the **Element Catalog**, insert **TextFormatRules**.

   A **TextFormatRules** element appears.
4. Insert **AllContextsRule**.

   An **AllContextsRule** element appears.
5. Insert **ParagraphFormatting**.

   A **ParagraphFormatting** element appears.
6. Specify **SpaceBelow** of `50 pt`.
   a. Insert **PropertiesBasic**.
   b. Insert **ParagraphSpacing**.
   c. Insert **SpaceBelow** and type: `50 pt`

7. Specify an **Angle** of **Italic** and **Size** of 20 points.

   a. Click below **PropertiesBasic** element, on line descending from the **ParagraphFormatting** element.

   b. Insert **PropertiesFont**.

   c. Insert **Angle**.

   The **Angle** element and an **Italic** child element appear.

   d. Click below the **Angle** element.

   e. Insert **Size** and type: `20 pt`

8. Specify a **Double Line** frame below.

   a. Click below **PropertiesFont** element, on the line descending from the **ParagraphFormatting** element.

   b. Insert **PropertiesAdvanced**.

   c. Insert **FrameBelow** and type:
   `Double Line`

   Double Line is the label of a frame on the reference page in your structured template.

9. Specify an **AutonumberFormat** of
   `C:Chapter <$chapnum>.`
   followed by a space

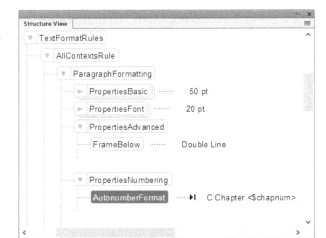

   a. Click below the **PropertiesAdvanced** element, on the line descending from the **ParagraphFormatting** element.

   b. Insert **PropertiesNumbering**.

   c. Insert **AutonumberFormat** and type:
   `C:Chapter <$chapnum>.` followed by a space.

10. Save your changes.

11. IMPORT AND CONFIRM THAT:

The Title element:

- Has 50 points below
- Is italic with a font size of 20 points
- Has an autonumber displaying as "Chapter 1. "
- Has a double line below

Chapter 1. [[Title Text]

[[Section Head]

[Para Text]]]

Exercise 4:   Specifying an AllContextsRule Referring to a FormatChangeList

In this exercise, you will specify an **AllContextsRule** for the **Head** element, that refers to a **FormatChangeList** called **HeadTitleText**, by inserting:

- **TextFormatRules** element
- **AllContextsRule** element
- **ParagraphFormatting** element
- **FormatChangeListTag** element and typing the tag as `HeadTitleText`

1. In the EDD, locate the **Head** element definition.

2. In the **Structure View**, click below the **AttributeList** for the **Head** element.

3. From the **Element Catalog**, insert **TextFormatRules**.

   TextFormatRules element appears.

4. Insert **AllContextsRule**.

   An **AllContextsRule** element appears.

5. Insert **ParagraphFormatting**.

   ParagraphFormatting element appears.

6. Insert **FormatChangeListTag**.

   FormatChangeListTag element appears.

7. In **FormatChangeListTag** element, type: `HeadTitleText`

8. Save your changes.

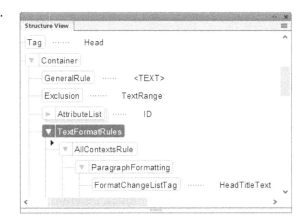

Exercise 5: Defining a FormatChangeList

In this exercise, you will define the **FormatChangeList** called **HeadTitleText** with a **Weight** of **Bold** and **SpaceAboveChange** of 5 pt, by inserting:

- **FormatChangeList** element and typing the **Tag** as **HeadTitleText**
- **PropertiesFont** element
- **Weight** element
- **Bold** element
- **PropertiesBasic** element
- **ParagraphSpacing** element
- **SpaceAboveChange** element and typing the space as +5 pt

Elements referencing this list of format changes will be bold, with an additional 5 points of space above them, added to whatever space they have already inherited.

1. In the EDD, place your cursor at the end of the **ElementCatalog** element.

   For ease of use, it is often best to define **FormatChangeList** elements at the end of the EDD, below all **Element** definitions.

2. From the **Element Catalog**, insert **FormatChangeList**.

   A **FormatChangeList** element and **Tag** child element appear.

3. In the **Tag** element, type: HeadTitleText

4. Specify a **Weight** of **Bold**.

   a. Click below **Tag** element, on line descending from **FormatChangeList** element.

   b. Insert **PropertiesFont**.

   c. Insert **Weight**.

   d. Insert **Bold**.

5. Specify a **SpaceAboveChange** of +5 pt.

   a. Click below **PropertiesFont** element, on line descending from **FormatChangeList** element.

   b. Insert **PropertiesBasic**.

   c. Insert **ParagraphSpacing**.

   d. Insert **SpaceAboveChange** and type: +5 pt

6. Save your changes.

7. IMPORT AND TEST.

   The **Head** element:

- Is bold
- Has an additional 5 points of space above, for a total of 15

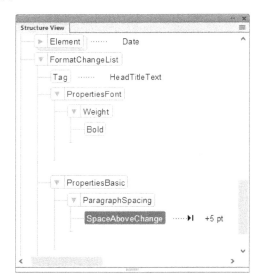

Exercise 6:   Specifying a Second AllContextsRule

In this exercise, you will specify a second **AllContextsRule** for the **Title** element. The second rule will refer to the **FormatChangeList** which makes the text bold and adds 5 points of space above the element.

A **FormatChangeList** applies only the formatting properties applicable to the particular context. Because the **Title** element is the first element containing text in the entire structure, **Title** falls at the top of the text column. White space above a paragraph falling at the top of a text column is ignored. Therefore, the **FormatChangeList** will only apply bold, not any additional space to the **Title** element.

1. In the EDD, locate the **Title** element definition.

2. In the **Structure View**, click below the **AllContextsRule** for the **Title** element, on the line descending from **TextFormatRules**.

3. Refer to the **FormatChangeList** tagged **HeadTitleText**.

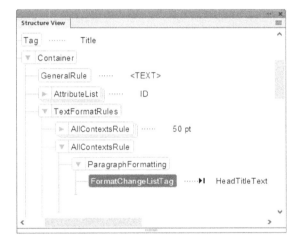

   a. Insert **AllContextsRule**.

   b. Insert **ParagraphFormatting**.

   c. Insert **FormatChangeListTag**

   d. In FormatChangeListTag element, type:
      `HeadTitleText`

4. Save your changes.

5. IMPORT AND TEST.

   The **Title** element:

- Is bold

- Does not have an as additional 5 points of space above, because it falls at the top of the text column

Exercise 7:   Specifying an AllContextsRule Referring to Text-Range Properties

In this exercise, you will specify an **AllContextsRule** for the **TextRange** element, identifying it as a text range with a font change of italics, by inserting:

- **TextFormatRules** element
- **AllContextsRule** element
- **TextRangeFormatting** element
- **PropertiesFont** element
- **Angle** element

Defining **TextRange** in the EDD as a text range will allow it to be embedded within a paragraph-type element without breaking the text into two paragraphs.

1. In the EDD, locate the **TextRange** element definition.

2. In the **Structure** View, click below the **GeneralRule** of the **TextRange** element.

3. From the **Element Catalog**, insert **TextFormatRules**.

   A **TextFormatRules** element appears.

4. Insert **AllContextsRule**.

   An **AllContextsRule** element appears.

5. To specify text-range formatting, rather than paragraph formatting, insert **TextRangeFormatting**.

   A **TextRangeFormatting** element and **TextRange** child element appear.

6. Specify an **Angle** of **Italic**.

   a. Insert **PropertiesFont**.

   b. Insert **Angle**.

      An **Angle** element and **Italic** child element appear.

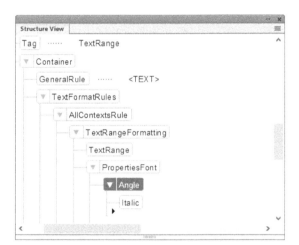

7. Save your changes.

8. IMPORT AND TEST.

   The **TextRange** element:

   - Is italic
   - No longer causes a break when inserted in a paragraph

   [Para text before TextRange. [*TextRange text*] Para text after TextRange.]

Exercise 8:　Formatting Captions with Two Rules

In this exercise, you will format the **Caption** for the **Graphic** (both children of **Figure**) by specifying two **AllContextsRules**:

- One refers to the **FormatChangeList**
- One specifies autonumbering of F:Figure <n+>. followed by a space

1. In the EDD, locate the **Caption** element definition.

2. In the **Structure View**, click below **GeneralRule** for the **Caption** element.

3. Insert **TextFormatRules**.

4. Attempt the rest on your own, referring to the picture.

5. Save your changes.

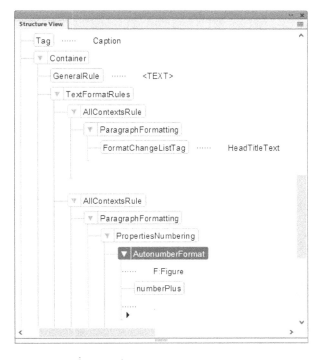

6. IMPORT AND TEST.

   The Caption element:

   · Is bold

   · Has an additional 5 points of space above, for a total of 15

   · Has an autonumber prefix displaying as "Figure 1. "

Figure 1. [[Figure Caption text]]

Exercise 9:　Formatting TableTitle Text

Tables do not inherit their formatting from their ancestors. Table parts inherit formatting from their ancestor table parts, up to the **Table** element. For example, formatting specified for:

- **Table** element passes to all descendants of the **Table** element
- **TableTitle** element passes to text and children of **TableTitle**
- **TableHeading** element passes to **TableRow** elements in the **TableHeading** and any **TableCells** in the **TableRows** of **TableHeading** only
- **TableBody** element passes to **TableRow** elements in the **TableBody** and any **TableCells** in the **TableRows** of **TableBody** only
- **TableFooting** element passes to **TableRow** elements in the **TableFooting** and any **TableCells** in the **TableRows** of **TableFooting** only

- TableRow element passes to its TableCell elements
- TableCell element passes to text and children of TableCell

Without format rules, text in the table is formatted according to the properties of the table format specified in its InitialTableFormat (or by any other table format the user chooses from the Insert Table dialog upon inserting the Table element). Table formats have default paragraph formats defined for use in the table title and cells of the table: TableTitle, CellHeading, CellBody, CellFooting.

In this exercise, you will format the TableTitle for the PartsTable with one AllContextsRule specifying two properties:

- Alignment of Left
- Autonumbering of T:Table <n+>. followed by a space

1. In the EDD, locate the `TableTitle` element definition.

2. In the **Structure View**, click below the **GeneralRule** of the **TableTitle** element.

3. Insert **TextFormatRules**.

4. Attempt the rest on your own, referring to the picture.

5. Save your changes.

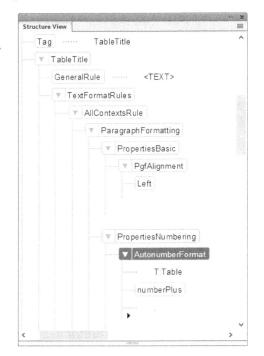

6. IMPORT AND TEST.

    The **TableTitle** element:

- Is left-aligned
- Has an autonumber displaying as "**Table 1.** "

Table 1. Table Title

Chapter 11: ContextRule formatting rules

Introduction

Objectives

- Write a:
  - ContextRule with If, ElseIf, Else clauses
  - LevelRule with If, ElseIf, Else clauses
- Analyze syntax for naming ancestors, siblings and attribute values
- Define subRules and multiple rules
- Write a ContextLabel
- Define a FormatChangeListLimits

Overview

ContextRule is an optional part of element definitions for:

- Container
- Table, TableTitle, TableHeading, TableBody, TableFooting, TableRow, TableCell
- Footnote

Identifies formatting for text in element:

- Rules for Table, TableHeading, TableBody, TableFooting, TableRow specify formatting only for text in descendant TableTitle and TableCell elements
- Changes are considered overrides
- When user reimports element definitions, user can keep or remove overrides

Writing a ContextRule

Defines one or more possible contexts, with format for each context

- Can have separate clauses for different possibilities
  - If—only one
  - ElseIf—zero or more
  - Else—zero or one

Each If, ElseIf, and Else clause specifies formatting changes, referring to:

- Named ParagraphFormatTag or CharacterFormatTag (if text range) stored in document
- Individual paragraph or text-range formatting properties
- Or FormatChangeList

ContextRule—Naming Ancestors

Naming just parent

- If **Item** element is within **List** element (regardless of **List**'s ancestors)

  Element (Container): Item
  > General rule: <TEXT>
  > Text format rules
  >> 1.   If context is: List
  >>> Numbering properties
  >>>> Autonumber format: \b\t

Less-than-sign (<) for list of ancestors

- If **Item** is within **List** within **Preface** element (regardless of **Preface**'s ancestors)

  Else if **Item** is within **List** with **Chapter** element (regardless of **Chapter**'s ancestors)

  Element (Container): Item
  > General rule: <TEXT>
  > Text format rules
  >> 1.   If context is: List < Preface
  >>> Numbering properties
  >>>> Autonumber format: \b\t
  >>>> Character format: bulletsymbol
  >>> Else, if context is: List < Chapter
  >>> Numbering properties
  >>>> Autonumber format: <n+>\t

- If **Section** is within two or more **Section** elements

  Element (Container): Section
  > General rule: Head, Para+
  > Text format rules
  >> 1.   If context is: Section < Section

Asterisk (*) for unspecified number of successive ancestors

- If **Section** has parent of **Section** and another ancestor tagged **Section** any number of levels up (grandparent, great-grandparent)

  Element (Container): Section
  > General rule: Head, Para+
  > Text format rules
  >> 1.   If context is: Section < * < Section

OR indicators (|) to test specification for any ancestor in group

- If **Item** is within **List** that is within **Preface** or **Chapter**

  Element (Container): Item
  > General rule: <TEXT>
  > Text format rules
  >> 1.   If context is: List < (Preface | Chapter)

Exercise 1:   Specifying a ContextRule with One Clause Naming a Parent

In this exercise, you will specify a **ContextRule** for the **Section** element that indents a **Section** (and all its descendants) when nested within a parent **Section**, by inserting:

- **TextFormatRules** element
- **ContextRule** element and typing the **Specification** of **Section**
- **ParagraphFormatting** element
- **PropertiesBasic** element
- **Indents** element
- **LeftIndentChange** element and typing a change of `+.5 in`
- **FirstIndentRelative** element (relative to left indent in use) and typing a value of 0

Because you are using the "change" and "relative" elements, each nested level of **Section** with be indented .5 inches further than the previous:

- **Section** < **Chapter** not indented
- **Section** < **Section** indented .5 inch
- **Section** < **Section** < **Section** indented 1 inch, etc.

1. In the EDD, locate the **Section** element definition.

2. In the **Structure View**, click below **AutoInsertions** for the **Section** element.

3. From the **Element Catalog**, insert **TextFormatRules**.

   A **TextFormatRules** element appears.

4. Insert **ContextRule**.

   ContextRule, **If**, and **Specification** elements appear.

5. In the **Specification** element, type:
   `Section`

6. Click below **Specification** element.

7. Specify **LeftIndentChange** of .5 in and **FirstIndentRelative** of 0

   a.   Insert **ParagraphFormatting**.

   b.   Insert **PropertiesBasic**.

   c.   Insert **Indents**.

   d.   Insert **LeftIndentChange** and type: `+.5 in`

   e.   Click below **LeftIndentChange** element.

   f.   Insert **FirstIndentRelative** and type: 0

8. Save your changes.

9. IMPORT AND TEST.

   The **Section** element (and all its descendants) is progressively indented in .5 inch increments.

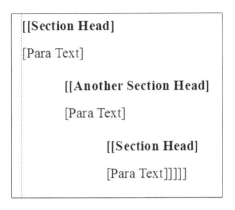

Exercise 2:   Indenting Lists

In this exercise, you will indent your **List** elements (and all their descendants) by specifying a **LeftIndentChange** of .25 inch and **FirstIndentRelative** of zero.

Because you are using the "change" and "relative" elements, indenting of **List** elements is added to the indenting of **Section** elements:

- **List < Section < Chapter** indented .25 inch
- **List < Section < Section** indented .75 inch
- **List < Section < Section < Section** indented 1.25 inches, etc.

To indent your lists:

1. In the EDD, locate the **List** element definition.

2. In the **Structure View**, click below **AutoInsertions** for the **List** element.

3. From the **Element Catalog**, insert **TextFormatRules**.

   A **TextFormatRules** element appears.

4. Insert **AllContextsRule**.

   An **AllContextsRule** element appears.

5. Specify **LeftIndentChange** of .25 in and **FirstIndentRelative** of 0

   a. Insert **ParagraphFormatting**.

   b. Insert **PropertiesBasic**.

   c. Insert **Indents**.

   d. Insert **LeftIndentChange** and type: `+.25 in`

   e. Click below **LeftIndentChange** element.

   f. Insert **FirstIndentRelative** and type: `0`

6. Save your changes.

7. IMPORT AND TEST.

The List element (and all its descendants) is indented in .25 inch more than its parent Section element.

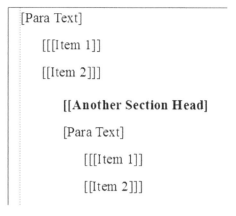

Exercise 3:   Specifying a ContextRule with Two Clauses Naming a Parent

In this exercise, you will specify **If** and **Else** clauses for the **WarnNote**, making it bold when a child of **Section** and italic when a child of **Item**.

To specify a context rule that will do this:

1. In the EDD, locate the **WarnNote** element definition.

2. In the **Structure View**, click below **AttributeList** of the **Section** element.

3. From the **Element Catalog**, insert **TextFormatRules**.

    A **TextFormatRules** element appears.

4. Insert **ContextRule**.

    A **ContextRule**, **If**, and **Specification** element each appear.

5. In **Specification** element, type: `Section`

6. Click below **Specification** element.

7. Specify Weight of Bold.

    a. Insert **ParagraphFormatting**.

    b. Insert **PropertiesFont**.

    c. Insert **Weight**.

    d. Insert **Bold**.

8. Click below If element, on line descending from ContextRule element.

9. Insert **Else**.

    Else element appears.

10. Specify Angle of **Italic**.

    a. Insert **ParagraphFormatting**.

    b. Insert **PropertiesFont**.

    c. Insert **Angle**.

11. Save your changes.

12. IMPORT AND TEST.

    The **WarnNote** element:

    - Is bold if a child of **Section**

    - Is otherwise italic

[[Section Head]

[Para Text]

[WarnNote (child of Section)]

   [[[Item 1]

    [WarnNote (child of Item)]]]]]

ContextRule—Naming Siblings and Naming Attribute Values

Sibling indicators describe relationship of:

- An element to its siblings

- An ancestor element to its siblings

Indicator	Specification is true if element is
{first}	First element in its parent
{middle}	Neither first element nor last element in its parent
{last}	Last element in its parent
{notfirst}	Not first element in its parent
{notlast}	Not last element in its parent
{only}	Only element in its parent
{before *sibling*}	Followed by named element or text content
{after *sibling*}	Preceded by named element or text content
{between *sibling1, sibling2*}	Between named elements or text content
{any}	Anywhere in its parent (equivalent to no indicator)

Current element to its siblings

- If **Item** is first child of its parent **NumberList**

    Element (Container): Item
        General rule: <TEXT>
        Text format rules
            1.   If context is: {first} < NumberList

Ancestor element to its siblings

- If **Head** is child of **Section** which is child of **Chapter**, and only if **Section** immediately follows a sibling **Title**

    Element (Container): Head
        General rule: <TEXT>
        Text format rules
            1.   If context is: Section {after Title} < Chapter

Attribute indicators describe context based on:

- Attribute name/value pair of current element
- Attribute name/value pair of ancestor element
- Set of attribute name/value pairs
- Operators with attribute name/value pairs

Attribute name/value pair of current element

- **Note** formatting based on **Label** attribute value

    Element (Container): Note
        General rule: <TEXT>
        Attribute list
            1.   Name: Label   Choice   Required
                 Choices: Important, Note, Tip
        Text format rules
            1.   If context is: [Label = "Important"]
                 Default font properties
                     Color: Red
                 Else, if context is: [Label = "Note"]
                 Default font properties
                     Weight: Bold
            Else
                 Default font properties
                     Angle: Italic

Attribute name/value pair of ancestor element

- If **Item** is within **List** where **Type** attribute of **List** has value of **Bullet**
- Else if **Item** is within **List** where **Type** attribute of **List** has value of **Numbered**

    Element (Container): Item
        General rule: <TEXT>
        Text format rules
            1.   If context is: List [Type = "Bullet"]
                 Numbering properties
                     Autonumber format: \b\t
                     Character format: bulletsymbol
                 Else, if context is: List [Type = "Numbered"]
                 Numbering properties
                     Autonumber format: <n+>\t

Set of name/value pairs, separated with ampersand (&)

- If **Item** is within **List** where Type attribute of **List** has value of **Num** and **Content** attribute has value of **Process**

    Element (Container): Item
        General rule: <TEXT>
        Text format rules
            1.   If context is: List [Type="Num" & Content="Process"]

Operators with attribute name/value pairs

Operator	With attributes of
= (equal to)	All types
!= (not equal to)	All types
> (greater than)	Choice and numeric types
< (less than)	Choice and numeric types
>= (greater than or equal to)	Choice and numeric types
<= (less than or equal to)	Choice and numeric types

- If **Item** is within **List** where **Type** attribute of **List** does not have a value of **Numbered**

  Element (Container): Item
      General rule: <TEXT>
      Text format rules
         1.   If context is: List [Type != "Numbered"]

- Operators with **Choice** attributes evaluates name/value pair using order in list of values in EDD, "lowest value" being one on left

- If **Section** is within **Report** where **Security** attribute of **Report** is any value to the left of **Classified**

  Element (Container): Section
      General rule: Head, Para+
      Text format rules
         1.   If context is: Report [Security < "Classified"]

- If **Section** is within **Report** where **Version** attribute **Report** has a value is between 2 and 5, inclusive

  Element (Container): Section
      General rule: Head, Para+
      Text format rules
         1.   If context is: Report [Version >= "2" & Version <= "5"]

Exercise 4:   Formatting Paras Using Attribute Values and Sibling Indicators

In your current structure, you can have two types of lists, **Bulleted** and **Numbered**, based of the **ListType** attribute value. List elements contain two or more **Item** elements. Item elements contain one or more **Para** elements.

In this exercise, you will specify two rules:

- One for the hanging indent and tab position whenever a **Para** is the first child of **Item**
- One for the numbering whenever a **Para** is the first child of **Item**:
  - In **List** elements with an attribute value **Bulleted**, regardless of the **Item** location in the List element (bullet symbol and tab)
  - In **List** elements with an attribute value **Numbered** but only if in the first **Item** in the **List** (restarting of autonumber **<n=1>** and **tab**)
  - In **List** elements of attribute value **Numbered** but only if not in the first **Item** in the **List** (continuing of autonumber **<n+>** and **tab**)

In a later exercise, you'll see how to simplify this formatting with a **SubRule**, but for now:

1. In the EDD, locate the **Para** element definition.

2. In the **Structure View**, click below the **GeneralRule** of the **Para** element.

3. From the **Element Catalog**, insert **TextFormatRules**.

   TextFormatRules element appears.

4. Insert **ContextRule**.

   A **ContextRule**, **If**, and **Specification** element all appear.

5. In **Specification** element, type:
   `{first} < Item`

6. Click below **Specification** element.

7. Specify **FirstIndentRelative** of `-.25 in` and **RelativeTabStopPosition** of `0`

   a. Insert **ParagraphFormatting**.

   b. Insert **PropertiesBasic**.

   c. Insert **Indents**.

   d. Insert **FirstIndentRelative** and type: `-.25 in`

   e. Click below **Indents** element.

   f. Insert **TabStops**.

   g. Insert **TabStop**.

   h. Insert **RelativeTabStopPosition** and type: `0`

8. Click below **ContextRule** element.

9. Insert another **ContextRule**.

   ContextRule, **If** and **Specification** elements appear.

10. In **Specification** element, type:
    `{first} < Item < List`
    `[ListType = "Bulleted"]`

11. Click below **Specification** element.

12. Specify **AutonumberFormat** of `\b\t`

    a. Insert **ParagraphFormatting**.

    b. Insert **PropertiesNumbering**.

    c. Insert **AutonumberFormat**.

    d. Insert **Bullet**.

    e. Insert **Tab**.

13. Click below **If** element.

14. Insert **ElseIf**.

    An **ElseIf** and a **Specification** element appear.

15. In **Specification** element, type:
    `{first} < Item {first} < List [ListType = "Numbered"]`

16. Click below **Specification** element.

17. Specify AutonumberFormat of `<n=1>.\t`

    a. Insert **ParagraphFormatting**.

    b. Insert **PropertiesNumbering**.

    c. Insert **AutonumberFormat**.

    d. Insert **numberFirst**.

    e. Type a period.

    f. Insert **Tab**.

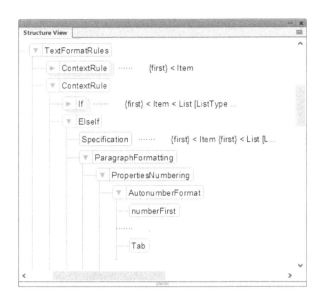

18. Click below ElseIf element.

19. Insert **ElseIf**.

    ElseIf and Specification elements appear.

20. In Specification element, type:
    `{first} < Item {notfirst} < List [ListType = "Numbered"]`

21. Click below Specification element.

22. Specify AutonumberFormat of `<n+>.\t`

    a. Insert **ParagraphFormatting**.

    b. Insert **PropertiesNumbering**.

    c. Insert **AutonumberFormat**.

    d. Insert **numberPlus**.

    e. Type a period.

    f. Insert **Tab**.

23. Save your changes.

24. IMPORT AND TEST.

    The **Para** element:

    - Has a bullet, tab and hanging indent when the first **Para** in any **Item** in a **List** of **ListType Bulleted**

    - Displays with "1.", with a tab and hanging indent when the first **Para** in the first **Item** in a **List** of **ListType Numbered**

    - Increments the "1." and displays with "2.", "3.", etc., with a tab and hanging indent when the first **Para** in an additional **Item** in a **List** of **ListType Numbered**

[[Section Head]

[Para before list]

1. [[[Item 1 Numbered]

   [WarnNote (child of Item)]]

2. [[Item 2 Numbered]]]

   [[Section Head]

   [Para before list]

   - [[[Item 1 bulleted]]

   - [[Item 1 bulleted]]]]]]

Exercise 5:   Controlling FrameMaker Behavior Using Attribute Values

In this exercise, you will use the attribute value of the **ReadyToImport** attribute on the **Figure** element to determine which dialog (**Import File** or **Anchored Frame**) appears when you insert **Graphic** elements.

1. In the EDD, locate the **Graphic** element definition.

2. In the **Structure View**, select the **AllContextsRule** element.

3. Press **Delete** to delete the **AllContextsRule**.

4. Insert **ContextRule**.

   A **ContextRule**, an **If**, and a **Specification** element appear.

5. In the **Specification** element, type:
   `Figure [ReadyToImport = "Yes"]`

6. Click below **Specification**.

7. Insert **ImportedGraphicFile**.

8. Click below **If**.

9. Insert **Else**.

10. Insert **AnchoredFrame**.

11. Save your changes.

12. IMPORT AND TEST.

    The Graphic element:

    - Displays the **Import File** dialog when in a **Figure** with an **ReadyToImport** attribute value of Yes

    - Displays the **Anchored Frame** dialog when in a **Figure** with an **ReadyToImport** attribute value of No

Writing a LevelRule

Defines formatting change when element is nested a specified number of levels in an ancestor

- In a **ContextRule**, **Section** < **Section** < **Section** means "nested in at least three Section elements"
- In a **LevelRule**, **Section** count of 3 means "nested in exactly three **Section** elements"
- Can also count instances of current element in hierarchy without specifying the ancestor
- Can have separate clauses for different levels
    - **If**—only one
    - **ElseIf**—zero or more
    - **Else**—zero or one

Each If, ElseIf, and Else clause specifies formatting changes, referring to:

- Named **ParagraphFormatTag** or **CharacterFormatTag** (if text range) stored in document
- Individual paragraph or text-range properties
- Or **FormatChangeList**

Exercise 6:   Numbering Headings Using LevelRules

In this exercise, you will specify numbering for **Head**, based on nesting level in **Section** ancestors.

1. In the EDD, locate the **Head** element definition.
2. In the **Structure View**, click below **AllContextsRule** for the **Head** element, on the line descending from **TextFormatRules**.
3. Insert **LevelRule**.

    The **LevelRule** element and **CountAncestors** child elements appear.
4. In **CountAncestors** element, type: `Section`
5. Click below **CountAncestors** element.
6. Insert **If**.

    The **If** element and **Specification** child elements appear.
7. In **Specification** element,
    type: `1`
8. Specify **ParagraphFormatting** of
    `C:<$chapnum>.<n+>.` followed by a space

    a. Click below **Specification** element.

    b. Insert **ParagraphFormatting**.

    c. Insert **PropertiesNumbering**.

    d. Insert **AutonumberFormat**.

    e. Type: `C:<$chapnum>.`

    f. Insert **numberPlus**.

    g. Type a period and space.

9. Click below **If** element.

10. Insert **ElseIf**.

    The **ElseIf** and **Specification** child elements appear.

11. In **Specification** element, type: 2

12. Specify **ParagraphFormatting** of
    C:<$chapnum>.<n>.<n+>.
    followed by a space

    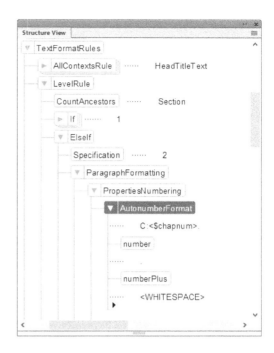

    a. Click below the **Specification** element.

    b. Insert **ParagraphFormatting**.

    c. Insert **PropertiesNumbering**.

    d. Insert **AutonumberFormat**.

    e. Type: C:<$chapnum>.

    f. Insert **number**.

    g. Type a period.

    h. Insert **numberPlus**.

    i. Type a period and space.

13. Click below **ElseIf** element.

14. Insert another **ElseIf**.

    ElseIf element and **Specification** child element appear.

15. In **Specification** element, type: 3

16. Specify **ParagraphFormatting** of
    C:<$chapnum>.<n>.<n>.<n+>. followed by a space

    a. Click below **Specification** element.

    b. Insert **ParagraphFormatting**.

    c. Insert **PropertiesNumbering**.

    d. Insert **AutonumberFormat**.

    e. Type: C:<$chapnum>.

    f. Insert **number**.

    g. Type a period.

    h. Insert **number**.

    i. Type a period.

    j. Insert **numberPlus**.

    k. Type a period and space.

17. Click below **ElseIf** element.

125

18. Insert **Else**.

    An **Else** element appears without **Specification** element.

19. Specify **ParagraphFormatting** of
    `DO NOT INDENT TO THIS LEVEL`
    using the **Color** Red.

    a. Insert **ParagraphFormatting**.

    b. Insert **PropertiesNumbering**.

    c. Insert **AutonumberFormat**.

    d. Type: `DO NOT INDENT TO THIS LEVEL`

    e. Click below **PropertiesNumbering**.

    f. Insert **PropertiesFont**.

    g. Insert **Color**.

    h. Type: `Red`

20. Save your changes.

21. IMPORT AND TEST:

    The **Head** element:

    · When nested within only one **Section**, displays an autonumber, based on the autonumber of the **Title** element, of "1.1.", "1.2.", etc.

    · When nested within two **Section** elements, displays an autonumber, based on the autonumber of the parent **Section** element, of "1.1.1.", "1.1.2.", etc.

    · When nested within three **Section** elements displays an autonumber, based on the parent **Section** element, of "1.1.1.1.", "1.1.1.2.", etc.

    · When nested within more than three **Section** elements, displays an autonumber, in red, of "**DO NOT INDENT TO THIS LEVEL**".

Chapter 1. [[Title Text]

1.1. [[Section Head]

[Para text]

    1.1.1 [[Section Head]

    [Para text]

        1.1.1.1 [[Section Head]

        [Para text]

            DO NOT INDENT TO THIS LEVEL[[Section Head]

            [Para text]]]]

Using Context Labels

Element definition can have context labels:

- In some dialoges, FrameMaker displays list of element tags for user to select from

  Example: User selects element tags in **Set Up** dialog (**Generate** command) to set up generated file such as index or table of contents

- You may want to distinguish among instances of some elements in these lists

  Example: User might include **Head** elements in table of contents when parent of **Head** is first- or second-level **Section**, but not when parent is more deeply nested **Section**

- In dialogs, user sees elements with context labels and a default group for all contexts in which no label applies

- Context labels cannot contain white-space characters or any of these special characters:

  ( ) & | , * + ? < > % [ ] = ! ; : { } "

Exercise 7:   Providing ContextLabels for Headings

In this exercise, you will specifying context labels for **Head**, based on its nesting level in **Section** ancestors.

1. In the EDD, locate the **Head** element definition.

2. In the **Structure View**, click below the **Specification** element for the first **If** clause.

3. From the **Element Catalog**, insert ContextLabel.

    A **ContextLabel** element appears.

4. In ContextLabel element, type:
    `SectionHead1`

5. In the **Structure View**, click below the Specification element for the first ElseIf clause.

6. Insert **ContextLabel**.

    ContextLabel element appears.

7. In ContextLabel element, type:
    `SectionHead2`

8. In the **Structure View**, click below the Specification element for the second ElseIf clause.

9. Insert **ContextLabel**.

    ContextLabel element appears.

10. In ContextLabel element, type:
    `SectionHead3`

11. Save your changes.

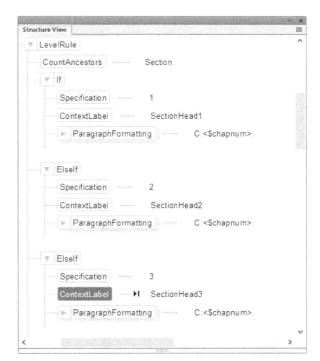

12. IMPORT AND TEST:

The Head element, when referred to from a dialog, such as the Cross-Reference dialog shown below, uses the following context labels to identify one level of Head from another level:

- SectionHead1 for Head elements nested within only one Section

- SectionHead2 for Head elements nested within exactly two Section elements

- SectionHead3 for Head elements nested within exactly three Section elements

- Otherwise, no label

Optional Exercise

Exercise 8:   Writing a SubRule for Paras in Items in Lists

In this exercise, you will revise the **TextFormatRules** for a **Para** in an **Item** in a **List** of **ListType** of **Numbered** by substituting an **ElseIf** clause with a **SubRule** for two **ElseIf** clauses.

1. In the EDD, locate the **Para** element definition.

2. In the **Structure View**, select the two **ElseIf** elements in the second **ContextRule** element.

3. Press **Delete** to delete the two **ElseIf** elements.

4. Rewrite the formatting rules, using one **ElseIf** with a **SubRule**, referring to the following pictures.

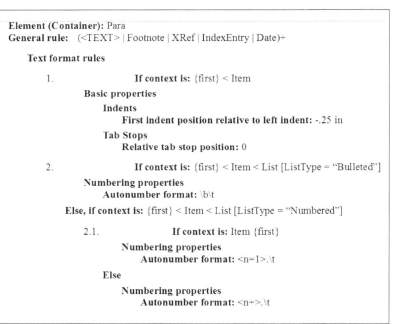

5. Save your changes.

6. IMPORT AND TEST.

The Para element is formatted exactly as before, just using a different method of writing the formatting specifications:

*   Has a bullet, tab and hanging indent when the first Para in any Item in a List of ListType Bulleted

*   Displays with "1.", with a tab and hanging indent when the first Para in the first Item in a List of ListType Numbered

*   Increments the "1." and displays with "2.", "3.", etc., with a tab and hanging indent when the first Para in an additional Item in a List of ListType Numbered

Chapter 1. Chapter Title

1.1. Section Head

Para text

*   Item bulleted

    Second Para in item

*   Item bulleted

    Second Para in item

Para text

1. Item numbered

    Second Para in item

2. Item numbered

    Second Para in item

Chapter 12: First/LastParagraphRules

Introduction

This chapter focuses on the formatting rules for first and last paragraphs in an element.

Objectives

- Specify **FirstParagraphRules** for formatting
- Specify **LastParagraphRules** for formatting
- Review difference between using **First/LastParagraphRules** and specifying {first}/{last} sibling indicators

Overview

Optional part of element definitions for Container elements only

- Applies special set of format rules to first or last paragraph in an element
- Ignored when first/last child element is formatted as a text range
- If element has prefix formatted in separate paragraph, prefix is first paragraph
- If element has suffix formatted in separate paragraph, suffix is last paragraph

You can specify First/LastParagraphRules with:

- AllContextsRule
- ContextRule
- LevelRule

Specifying First/LastParagraphRules

Exercise 1:   Specifying Formatting Properties with First/Last Rules

In this exercise, you will specify that the last paragraph in a **List** element will have extra space below it, regardless if that paragraph is in a **WarnNote**, **Para**, or other element.

1. If it is not already open, from your class files directory, open EDD.fm, the EDD you'll be modifying throughout the class.

   If you did not finish the previous chapter's modifications to the EDD, please open **Chapter 12-start First Last Paras.fm** instead, and save it in your class files directory as EDD.fm.

If needed, download the class files by visiting http://www.techcommtools.com/struct-auth-files/

2. In the EDD, locate the **List** element definition.

3. In the **Structure View**, click below the **TextFormatRules** element.

4. From the **Element Catalog**, insert **LastParagraphRules**.

   A **LastParagraphRules** element appears.

5. Insert **AllContextsRule**.

   An **AllContextsRule** element appears.

6. Insert **ParagraphFormatting**.

7. Insert **PropertiesBasic**.

8. Insert **ParagraphSpacing**.

9. Insert **SpaceBelow**.

10. In the **SpaceBelow** element,
    type: `15 pt`

11. Save your changes.

12. IMPORT AND TEST:

    The last paragraph in the **List** element, regardless if it is a descendant **Para** or **WarnNote**, has 15 points of space below.

    If you had specified **TextFormatRules** of **SpaceBelow** 15 points for the **List** element, rather than **LastParagraphRules**, each descendant **Item** and their children would have 15 points below, unless you wrote another rule counteracting that inheritance.

    If you had used {last} sibling indicators, you would have had to define the {last} sibling indicators for all potential last children.

1.1. Section Head

Para before list

• Item 1 bulleted

• Item 1 bulleted

Para below List

Chapter 13: PrefixRules and SuffixRules

Introduction

This chapter focuses on defining the **PrefixRules** and **SuffixRules** for **Container** elements.

Objectives

- Define prefix and suffix
- Specify **PrefixRules** and **SuffixRules** using fixed text string
- Specify **PrefixRules** and **SuffixRules** referring to attribute values
- Specify formatting for prefix and suffix
- Compare use of autonumbers, **Prefix/SuffixRules**, and **First/LastParagraphRules**

Overview

Optional part of element definitions for Container elements only

- A prefix is text range defined in EDD that appears at beginning of element (before element's content)
- A suffix is text range defined in EDD that appears at end of element (after content)
- **PrefixRules** and **SuffixRules** describe both text string and any special font properties
- Format rules for prefix/suffix describe font changes only for prefix/suffix

  Font changes do not apply to descendants
- If element has **FirstParagraphRules** and **LastParagraphRules** and prefix/suffix is formatted in a paragraph of its own, prefix/suffix is first/last paragraph for formatting
- Because **PrefixRules** and **SuffixRules** applied after first/last rules, **PrefixRules** and **SuffixRules** can override font changes in first/last rule

Examples:

Prefix/suffix for text range element inside a paragraph

- Result: Display double quotation marks around the text of a quotation

Element (Container): Quotation
    General rule: <TEXT>
    Text format rules
        1.   In all contexts.
                Text range.
    Prefix rules
        1.   In all contexts.
                Prefix: "
    Suffix rules
        1.   In all contexts.
                Suffix: "

Prefix/suffix for a paragraph, similar to autonumber

- Result: Display **Important:** at beginning of paragraph

Element (Container): Note
    General rule: <TEXT>
    Prefix rules
        1.   In all contexts.
                Prefix: Important:

Prefix/suffix for element with sequence of paragraphs

- Result: Display bold string **Synopsis and Contents**, **Arguments**, or **Examples** in paragraph by itself above First child Para

Element (Container): Syntax
    General rule: Para+
    Prefix rules
        1.   If context is: Synopsis
                Prefix: Synopsis and Contents
           Else, if context is: Args
                Prefix: Arguments
           Else, if context is: Examples
                Prefix: Examples
        2.   In all contexts.
                Text range.
                Font properties
                    Weight: Bold
    Format rules for first paragraph in element
        1.   In all contexts
                Basic properties
                    Paragraph spacing
                        Space below: 4pt

Format rules for first paragraph puts 4 points of space below the prefix paragraph

Prefix/suffix for both text range and paragraph

- Result: Display **AuthorNote** element within **Para** as text range, else as paragraph, with prefix/suffix

```
Element (Container): AuthorNote
      General rule: <TEXT>
      Text format rules
            1.    If context is: Para
                        Text range.
                        Font properties
                              Angle: Italic
                  Else
                        Default font properties
                        Angle: Italic
      Prefix rules
            1.    In all contexts.
                        Prefix:  [Author's comments:
                        Text range.
                              Font properties
                                    Weight: Bold
      Suffix rules
            1.    In all contexts.
                        Suffix: ]
                        Text range.
                              Font properties
                                    Weight: Bold
```

Using attribute values in PrefixRules and SuffixRules

- Result: Display value of **Security** attribute in current element

  Prefix: <$attribute[Security]>

- Result: Display value of **Security** attribute in closest ancestor **Item** or **LabelPara**

  Prefix: <$attribute[Security: Item, LabelPara]>

- Result: Display value of **Security** attribute in closest ancestor **Head** element with **Chapter Level** context label

  Prefix: <$attribute[Security: Head(Chapter Level)]>

Specifying PrefixRules and SuffixRules

Exercise 1:   Specifying Prefix Based on Attribute Value

In this exercise, you will use the **WarnNote** element's **MessageType** attribute value as a prefix for the element and apply to it the color **Red**.

1. If it is not already open, from your class files directory, open `EDD.fm`, the EDD you'll be modifying throughout the class.

   If you did not finish the previous chapter's modifications to the EDD, please open **Chapter 13-start Prefix Suffix.fm** instead, and save it in your class files directory as `EDD.fm`.

If needed, download the class files by visiting http://www.techcommtools.com/struct-auth-files/

2. In the EDD, locate the **WarnNote** element definition.

3. In the **Structure View**, click below the **TextFormatRules** element.

4. From the **Element Catalog**, insert **PrefixRules**.

   A **PrefixRules** element appears.

5. Insert **AllContextsRule**.

   An **AllContextsRule** element appears.

6. Insert **Prefix**.

   A **Prefix** element appears.

7. Insert **AttributeValue**.

   An **AttributeValue** element appears.

8. In the **AttributeValue** element, type:
   `MessageType`

9. Click below the **AttributeValue** element.

10. Type a colon (:) followed by a space.

11. Click below the **Prefix** element.

12. Insert **WarnNoteFormatting**.

13. Insert **PropertiesFont**.

14. Insert **Color**.

15. In the **Color** element, type: `Red`

16. Save your changes.

17. IMPORT AND TEST.

    The **WarnNote** element displays a red prefix of:

    - "**NOTE:** " if using **MessageType** attribute value NOTE.

    - "**WARNING:** " if using **MessageType** attribute value WARNING.

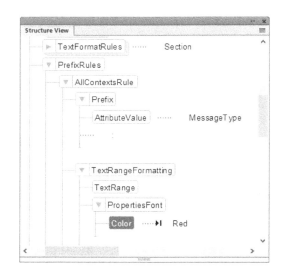

1.1. Section Head

Para before WarnNote

NOTE: **WarnNote (child of Item)**

Para before WarnNote

WARNING: |WarnNote (child of Item)

Exercise 2:   Specifying Quotation Marks Around a Text-Range Element

In this exercise, you will and both a **PrefixRule** and a **SuffixRule** to add quotation marks around the **TextRange** element.

1. In the EDD, locate the **TextRange** element definition.

2. In the **Structure View**, click below the **TextFormatRules** for the **TextRange** element.

3. Insert **PrefixRules**.

4. Attempt the rest on your own, referring to the picture below.

5. Save your changes.

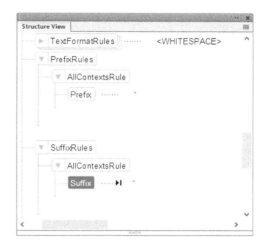

6. IMPORT AND TEST.

   The **TextRange** element has curved quotes around it in the Document View.

   Based on your system, you may want to specify straight quotes, or specific curved quote characters with FrameMaker character codes.

Chapter 1. Title Text

1.1. Section Head

Para containing a *"text range"* element.

Chapter 14: Elements for Structuring Books

Introduction

In this chapter, you will define book-related elements in the EDD, import them into a chapter in a book, generate the book, adding additional chapters, and a table of contents and index.

Objectives

- Define element for book
- Define elements for generated files within book
- Generate a structured book
- Add files to structured book
- Generate and format a table of contents
- Generate and format an index
- Wrap generated files into elements of structured book

Overview

Use books to:

- Maintain several documents as one larger document
- Generate table of contents, index, list of figures, list of tables for several files at once
- Allow page sides, page numbering, paragraph numbering to continue across files
- Open, save, print and close all files at once
- Enforce consistent structure of all files within book

A structured book has its own:

- Element hierarchy, which display in the Structure View
- List of elements, which display in the Element Catalog

A book's element definitions are:

Defined in same EDD shared by book's chapters

- They define a container element for the book and specify that it is ValidHighestLevel
- They define a container element for each structured file within the book and specify ValidHighestLevel
- They define a container element for each generated (unstructured) file within the book with a GeneralRule of <TEXT>

Defining and Testing Book Elements

Exercise 1:   Defining an Element for the Entire Book

In this exercise, you will define a **Container** element that is **ValidHighestLevel** for the book as a whole.

1. If it is not already open, from your class files directory, open **EDD.fm**, the EDD you'll be modifying throughout the class.

    If you did not finish the previous chapter's modifications to the EDD, please open
    Chapter 14-start Book Elements.fm instead, and save it in your class files directory as `EDD.fm`.

    If needed, download the class files by visiting http://www.techcommtools.com/struct-auth-files/

2. In the EDD, click on the line descending from the **ElementCatalog** element, anywhere above the **FormatChangeListLimits** element at the very end.

3. Insert another **Element** element and tag it **UserManual**.

    a. From the **Element Catalog**, insert an **Element** element.

        An **Element** element and a **Tag** child element appear.

    b. In the **Tag** element, type: `UserManual`

4. Define **UserManual** as a **Container** with a **GeneralRule** of
    `TOC, Chapter, Chapter+, IX?`

    a. Click below the **Tag** element.

    b. From the **Element Catalog**, insert **Container**.

        The **Container** element and a **GeneralRule** child element appear.

    c. In the **GeneralRule** element, type: `TOC, Chapter, Chapter+, IX?`

5. Define **UserManual** as **ValidHighestLevel**.

    a. Click above or below the **GeneralRule** element, on the line descending from the **Container** element.

    b. From the **Element Catalog**, insert **ValidHighestLevel**.

        ValidHighestLevel element and **Yes** child element appear.

6. Save your changes.

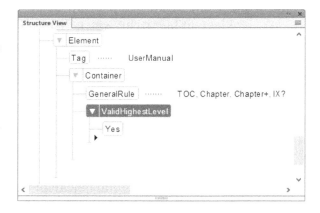

Exercise 2:   Defining Elements for the Generated Files

In this exercise, you will define **Container** elements for two generated file elements—**TOC** and **IX**.

1. Insert another **Element** element and tag it **TOC**.

   a. From the **Element Catalog**, insert an **Element** element.

      An **Element** element and a **Tag** child element appear.

   b. In the **Tag** element, type: `TOC`

2. Define **TOC** as a **Container** with a **GeneralRule** of `<TEXT>`

   a. Click below the **Tag** element.

   b. From the **Element Catalog**, insert **Container**.

      Container element and **GeneralRule** child element appear.

   c. In the **GeneralRule** element, type: `<TEXT>`

3. Insert another **Element** element and tag it `IX`.

   a. From the **Element Catalog**, insert an **Element** element.

      An **Element** element and a **Tag** child element appear.

   b. In the **Tag** element, type: `IX`

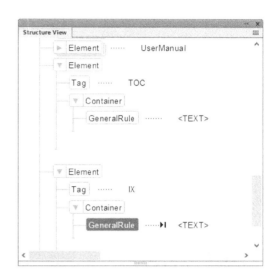

4. Define **IX** as a **Container** with a **GeneralRule** of `<TEXT>`

   a. Click below the **Tag** element.

   b. From the **Element Catalog**, insert **Container**.

      Container element and **GeneralRule** child element appear.

   c. In the **GeneralRule** element, type: `<TEXT>`

5. Save your changes.

Exercise 3:   Reimporting and Retesting

In this exercise, you will reimport the EDD into the structured template and test your element definitions for **UserManual**, **TOC**, and **IX**.

 Although you will not be using these elements in a single file, it is best to test them in the structured template before importing into the book.

1. Reimport your element definitions and fix any errors.

    a. In `testdoc.fm`, from the **File** menu, choose **Import > Element Definitions**.

        The **Import Element Definitions** dialog appears.

    b. From the **Import from Document** popup menu, choose `EDD.fm`.

    c. Click **Import**.

        An alert box appears indicating "**Element definitions have been imported from the EDD.**"

    d. Click **OK** to close the alert box.

    e. If you had errors in the element definitions, edit your EDD and reimport.

2. In the **Structure View**, select the **Chapter** element (at the top of the structure) and delete it.

    The **Element Catalog** displays the UserManual element as valid.

3. Insert a **UserManual** element.

    The **UserManual** is inserted, and the **Element Catalog** displays the **TOC** element as valid.

4. Insert **TOC**

    The **Element Catalog** displays **<TEXT>** as valid.

5. In the **Structure View**, click below the **TOC** element.

    The **Element Catalog** displays the **Chapter** element as valid.

6. Insert **Chapter** then click below it in the Structure View.

   The **Element Catalog** displays the **Chapter** element as valid again (you have to have two).

7. Insert **Chapter** then click below it in the Structure View.

   The **Element Catalog** displays the **Chapter** and **IX** elements as valid.

8. Insert **IX**.

   The **Element Catalog** displays **<TEXT>** as valid.

9. Save your changes.

While this structure looks like a book, it isn't as useful as the FrameMaker book structure you may be used to and the numbering isn't acting as we would expect.

In the rest of this lesson you will create a "normal" FrameMaker book with a generated TOC and Index.

Generating a FrameMaker Book

Exercise 4: Importing the Element Definitions into the Chapter

In this exercise, you will import your element definitions into a chapter from which you will then generate the book. The chapter is already structured, using the version of the EDD without the book definitions. Because you are importing into the chapter before generating the book, the book will automatically have the book's element definitions available in its **Element Catalog**.

1. From your class files directory, open **chap1.fm**.

   a. From the **File** menu, choose **Open**.

      The **Open** dialog appears.

   b. If necessary, change to your class files directory.

   c. Double-click **chap1.fm**.

      The sample structured document appears. This document already contains the full EDD needed to complete the exercises.

2. Save your changes.

Exercise 5:   Generating a Book

In this exercise, you will create and save a book.

1. With your cursor in the **chap1.fm** file, choose **File>New>Book** menu.

   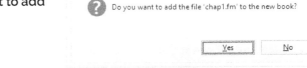

   An alert box appears asking "**Do you want to add the file'chap1.fm' to the new book?**"

2. Select the **Yes** button to proceed.

   A new book window appears.

   Notice that FrameMaker shows the path of the **chap1.fm** file, but not the path of the book.

   You will save the book to your disk. Afterward, the path of the book will show, and only a relative path to the **chap1.fm** file will remain.

3. With the book window active, choose **File> Save Book As**.

   The **Save Book** dialog appears.

4. In the **File name** text box, delete the contents and type: `UserManual.book`

   You can manually type in the **.book** extension, but FrameMaker will add it automatically if you forget.

5. Click **Save**.

   The book is now saved with its new name. Note the lack of a pathname for **chap1.fm** as it is stored in the same directory as **UserManual.book**.

Exercise 6:   Adding Files

In this exercise, you will add three more chapters to the book.

1. With the book window active, choose **Insert>Files**.

   The **Add Files to Book** dialog appears.

2. Select the **chap2.fm, chap3.fm** and **chap4.fm** files.

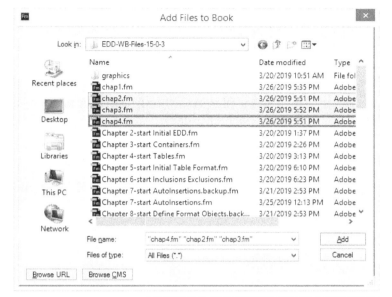

3. Click **Add**.

   The book window updates to display the added files. You'll rearrange the files in the next exercise.

4. With the book window active, from the **File** menu, choose **Save**.

Exercise 7:   Rearranging Files in the Book

In this exercise, you will rearrange the files in the book, putting the four chapters in numerical order. If your chapters are already in numerical order, skip to the next exercise.

1. Rearrange your files as needed by selecting and dragging individual files in either the book window or the structure window.

   You can also move their position by using the arrows above the book name.

2. Move all the files in the book until they are all in the correct order.

3. From the **File** menu, choose **Save**.

The **Structure View** displays the highest-level element as **NoName** and each file as **BOOK-COMPONENT**. You'll correct this in the next exercise.

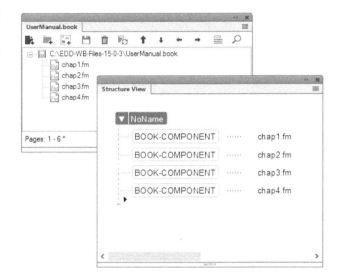

Exercise 8:   Changing NoName Into an Element

The **NoName** element at the top of the book window indicates that FrameMaker doesn't yet know what part of the structure should be applied here. In this exercise, you will change the **NoName** element into a **UserManual** element.

1. In the **Structure View**, select the **NoName** element.

2. From the **Element Catalog**, select **UserManual** and click **Change**.

   The **Structure View** now shows the highest-level element as **UserManual**.

3. Save your changes.

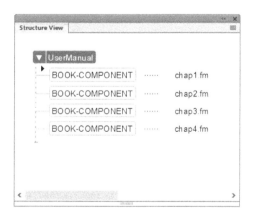

Exercise 9:   Updating the book to correct Chapter elements in Structure View

In this exercise, you will update the book. Before you update the book, you need to turn off element boundaries in each file. Element boundaries take up space and, therefore, affect the page breaks and page numbering throughout the book and its generated table of contents and index.

In FrameMaker 2015 and earlier, boundaries, text symbols, and other items were managed by individual documents. Starting with FrameMaker 2017, these settings are changed for all open documents. You'll start this exercise by opening all files in book to take advantage of this feature.

1. Ensure that the book window is the active document.

2. Shift+click on the **File** menu, and choose **Open all files in book**.

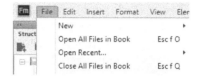

3. From the **View** menu, while a chapter file is the active document, turn off **Element Boundaries**.

    The **Element Boundaries** are now off in all four chapter files.

4. Shift+click the **File** menu again to choose **Save All Open Files** or **Save All Files in Book**.

    The choice you see depends on whether you had a chapter file or the book file active when you Shift+clicked the **File** menu.

5. With the book window active, choose **Edit>Update Book**, or use the **Update** button (🗐) in the book file.

    The **Update Book** dialog appears.

    Because you have not yet added any placeholders for generated files, nothing appears in the **Generate** and **Don't Generate** fields.

6. Click **Update**.

    Messages appear at the bottom of the book window showing the progress of the update.

    When done, the **Structure View** displays each file as **Chapter**, the highest-level element in each file.

7. With the book window active, shift+click the **File** menu, and choose **Save All Files in Book**.

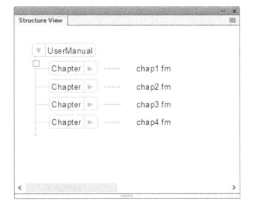

Exercise 10: Adding a Table of Contents

In this exercise, you will add a table of contents to the book. In the book window, each generated file will have a plus sign (+) following its name to indicate that it is a generated file.

1. In the Structure View for your book, click to the right of the missing content. (to the right of the red square)

2. Choose **Insert > Create Standalone TOC**.

   The **Setup Table of Contents** dialog appears.

   Because you selected **chap1.fm**, the default settings will place the TOC accurately. Otherwise, you might need to reposition the TOC in the future and regenerate for expected results.

3. Move the following elements to the **Include Elements/Paragraph Formats** scroll list:

   · Head (SectionHead1)

   · Head (SectionHead2)

   · Title

4. Turn on **Create Hypertext Links**.

   Hypertext links will be added to the table of contents, making the TOC clickable in PDF and other formats.

5. Click **OK**.

6. Click **Update**

The **TOC** has been added to the book, but is represented by the BOOK COMPONENT element in the **Structure View**. This unstructured FrameMaker document needs to be wrapped in an appropriate structured element; in this case, a **TOC** element.

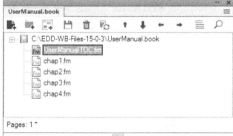

7. Select the **BOOK COMPONENT** in the book file **Structure View** and wrap it in a **TOC** element using the **Element Catalog.**

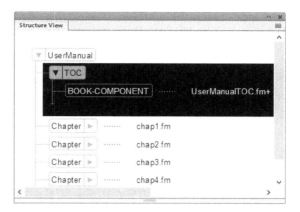

 As of the date of publishing, FrameMaker has a long-standing behavior of opening generated files like TOC and IX into their own window, rather than opening into the tabbed interface. If this happens to you, just drag the tab of your generated file into the other tabs for your project. You can also use the **Window > Consolidate** command to collect files into the standard tabbed interface.

Exercise 11: Adding an index

Your sample documents already contain index markers, so you just need to collect them using a generated index file in your book.

1. In the structure window, place your cursor at the end of the book.

2. Choose **Insert > Standard Index.** Change your settings to match the image, if needed.

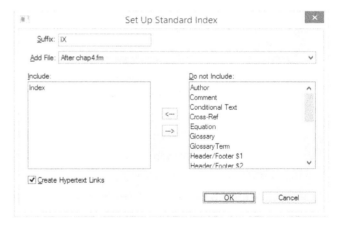

3. Click **OK**.

    The **Update Book** dialog appears.

    Make sure that both the **TOC** and **IX** files are in the **Generate** column.

4. Click **Update**.

    The book window updates to display a placeholder for the generated index.

    Notice the difference in color between the generated and non-generated files.

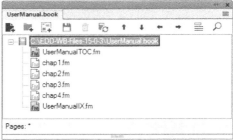

  Although the entries for the table of contents and the index appear in the book window, the generated files do not physically exist until the book is updated.

The **Structure View** displays the index as **BOOK-COMPONENT**.

Additionally, the **Structure View** shows a **+** at the end of the generated file filename snippets.

5. With the book window active, from the **File** menu, choose **Save**.

6. Select the **BOOK-COMPONENT** and wrap it in an **IX** element.

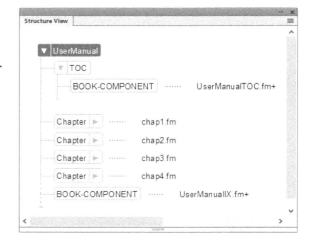

Exercise 12: Formatting a Table of Contents

In this exercise, you will open a table of contents template and save it with a new name in the book file's directory. This will result in an automatically formatted table of contents when you generate/update the book.

1. From your class files directory, open **toc.tpl.fm.**

   a. From the **File** menu, choose **Open.**

      The **Open** dialog appears.

   b. If necessary, change to your class files directory.

   c. Double-click **toc.tpl.fm.**

      The document appears.

2. Choose **File>Save As**, save the file as `UserManualTOC.fm` in your class files directory.

   The table of contents will be populated when you update the book in a later exercise.

 You can also use File>Import>Formats to import the toc.tpl.fm formats into the UserManualTOC.fm file.

 To learn more about formatting tables of contents, indexes, and other FrameMaker formatting options, see my reference book, *FrameMaker - Working with Content,* or consider taking my template design course. Information on both books and courses is available at www.techcommtools.com.

Exercise 13: Formatting an Index

In this exercise, you will open an index template and save it with a new name in the book file's directory.

1. From your class files directory, open **ix.tpl.fm.**

   a. From the **File** menu, choose **Open.**

      The **Open** dialog appears.

   b. If necessary, change to your class files directory.

   c. Double-click **ix.tpl.fm.**

      The document appears.

2. Using Save As, save **ix.tpl** as `UserManualIX.fm` in your class files directory.

   The index will be populated when you generate/update the book in the next exercise.

 You can also use File>Import>Formats to import the IX.tpl.fm formats into the UserManualTOC.fm file.

Exercise 14: Setting up the Book Files

In this exercise, you will set up the page side, page numbering, paragraph numbering, and prefix for each file in the book.

1. In the book window, right-click on **UserManualTOC.fm** and choose **Numbering**.

   The **Numbering Properties** dialog appears.

2. On the Page tab, match the **First Page #** and **Format** options as shown.

3. Click **Set**.

4. In the book window, right-click on **chap1.fm** and choose **Numbering**.

   a. On the Page tab, set properties as shown.

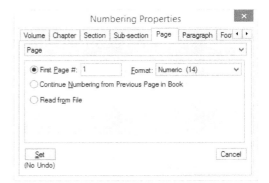

   b. On the Chapter tab set the properties as shown.

5. Click **Set**.

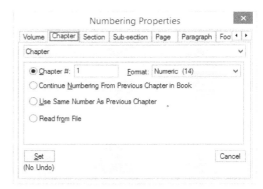

6. Select all the files after **chap1.fm** in the book window.

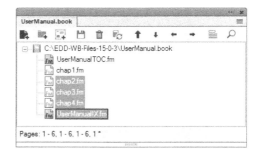

7. Right-click on the selected files and choose **Numbering**.

   a. On the **Chapter** tab, select the **Continue Numbering From Previous Chapter in Book** radio button.

   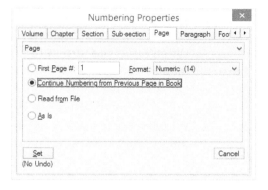

   b. Move to the **Page** tab and select the **Continue From Previous Page in Book** radio button.

8. Click **Set**.

Exercise 15: Update the Book

In this exercise, you will update the book to fix page sides and numbering and update paragraph numbering and populate the generated files.

1. Select the **Update** button (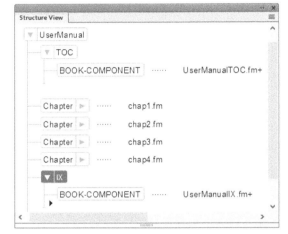) in the book file.

    The **Update Book** dialog appears.

2. Click **Update**.

    Messages appear at the bottom of the book window showing the progress of the update.

When done, the **Structure View** continues to display each file as **Chapter**, the highest-level element in each file, except for the generated files which still display as **BOOK-COMPONENT**.

3. With the book window active, shift-click the **File** menu, choose **Save All Files in Book**.

Exercise 16: Reviewing the Book Files

In this exercise, you will open and check the newly generated table of contents and index.

1. From the book window, double-click the table of contents file.

    The table of contents opens, already formatted because you saved the table of contents template with the correct file name.

2. Review the entries in the table of contents.

3. Close the table of contents.

4. From the book window, double-click the index file.

    The index opens, already formatted because you saved the index template with the correct file name.

5. Review the entries in the index.

6. Close the index.

7. From the book window, double-click each chapter, noticing the continuation of the chapter numbering across the files.

Chapter 15: Structuring Unstructured Data

Introduction

In this chapter, you will set up a conversion table and define object and element mapping in it. After defining the conversion table, you will use its mapping to add structure to unstructured documents.

Objectives

- Learn conversion rule syntax
- Generate conversion table
- Learn how to create conversion table from scratch
- Structure a currently unstructured document
- Structure a group of unstructured files
- Structure unstructured book

Overview

Two Ways to Wrap Unstructured Data

- Method 1—Manually, element by element. This method is only good for very small conversions.
- Method 2—Automatically, using the tools available in **Structured > Utilities**

Automatic wrapping requires a conversion table:

- Usually, created by application developer
- Provides table of mappings to automate the task of adding structure to unstructured documents
- Uses paragraph and character tags, and object types (such as equations or footnotes), to identify how to wrap document components in elements
- Also specifies how to wrap child elements in parent elements

Organization of conversion table itself:

- Regular table, with at least 3 columns and 1 body row
- Additional columns and heading/footing rows can hold comments
- Each body row holds 1 rule

Column 1	Column 2	Column 3
specifies document object, child element, or sequence to wrap	specifies element in which to wrap	specifies optional qualifier ("nickname") to use as temporary label

Organization of conversion table document:

- Conversion table can be split up into several tables with text or graphics in between for comments
- Cannot have any tables other than conversion tables
- Must be saved before it can be used

Rule Syntax—Character Restrictions

Case-Sensitivity in Tags:

- Format tags and element tags are case-sensitive and must be specified as defined in their catalogs
- Qualifier tags are case-sensitive and two occurrences of one qualifier must match exactly

Special characters in Tags:

( ) & | , * + ? % [ ] : \

- In format tags and qualifier tags—allowed but only if preceded by a backslash (\) in the table
- In element tags—not allowed

A space character in Tags:

- Does not need to be preceded with a backslash
- For example, you can write the tag Format A

Wildcard character (%) in Tags:

- Use % as in format or element tag to match zero, one, or more characters (similar to * in general rule)
- For example, P:%Body matches paragraphs with the format tag Body, FirstBody, or BulletBody

Methods for Producing a Conversion Table

- Method 1—FrameMaker Generates Initial Table (easiest, recommended, and is the method used in this course)
- Method 2—Create a conversion table from scratch (requires creating and populating entries for all catalog entries, and not recommended for most users)

Exercise 1:   Generating Initial Conversion Table

In this exercise, you will generate a conversion table from an unstructured document.

1. From your class files directory, open wraptest.fm.
    a. From the **File** menu, choose **Open**.

       The **Open** dialog appears.
    b. If necessary, change to your class files directory.
    c. Double-click wraptest.fm.

If needed, download the class files by visiting http://www.techcommtools.com/struct-auth-files/

The document appears.

> ### *Chapter 1. Side Doors¶*
>
> 1.1. Introduction¶
>
>   1.1.1. Chapter Overview¶
>
>   1.1.1.1. Procedures in This Chapter¶
>
>   This chapter describes maintenance procedures for the side doors on the Astro-Liner T440B and T442 light rail cars. It includes safety guidelines, an overview of door components, and a maintenance schedule for some of the components.¶
>
>   The procedures in this chapter cover disassembling and reinstalling door panels.[1]¶
>
>   1.1.1.2. Related Information¶
>
>   For information about routine operational testing, see *Chapter 5 of the manual Testing and Troubleshooting* in this volume, part number TT1-500 093. For detailed troubleshooting techniques that address specific side door problems, see *Chapter 18 of the same manual*.¶
>
>   1.1.2. Safety Guidelines¶
>
>   1.1.2.1. Basic Precautions¶
>
>   All maintenance personnel must wear approved protective clothing and follow the

2. Open the **Structure View** and **Element Catalog**.

   Both the **Structure View** and **Element Catalog** are blank because this is an unstructured document.

3. Scroll through the document, clicking in various paragraphs to identify the paragraph formats being used.

4. From the **File** menu, choose **Structure > Utilities > Generate Conversion Table**.

   The **Generate Conversion Table** dialog appears.

5. Select **Generate New Conversion Table** and click **Generate**.

A conversion table, based on your document's format tags, appears.

Wrap this object or objects	In this element	With this qualifier
P:Title	Title	
P:H1	H1	
P:H2	H2	
P:H3	H3	
P:Regular	Regular	
P:Bulleted	Bulleted	
P:Caption	Caption	
P:TableTitle	TableTitle	
P:Pname	Pname	
P:Pnum	Pnum	
P:Pcount	Pcount	
P:Indented	Indented	
P:StepFirst	StepFirst	
P:Step	Step	
P:Note	Note	
C:Emphasis	Emphasis	
C:WarnNote	WarnNote	
X:ElemNumTextPage	ElemNumTextPage	
M:Index	Index	
M:Cross-Ref	Cross-Ref	
G:	GRAPHIC	
F:flow	FOOTNOTE	
T:Format A	FormatA	
TT:	TITLE	
TH:	HEADING	
TB:	BODY	
TF:	FOOTING	
TR:	ROW	
TC:	CELL	

6. Use the **Save As** dialog to save this new untitled document into your class files directory with the new filename `Conversion Table.fm`

   a. From the **File** menu, choose **Save As.**

   The **Save Document** dialog appears.

   b. If necessary, change to your class files directory.

   c. In the **Save in File** field , delete the current file name and type: `Conversion Table.fm`

   d. Click **Save.**

Typing the Conversion Rules

In Column 1:

- Type a one- or two-letter code to identify the type of item
- Type a format (optional) to narrow the definition

For this object	Use this Code	Followed by optional
Paragraph	P:	Paragraph format tag
Text range	C:	Character format tag
Table	T:	Table format tag
Table title	TT:	(none)
Table heading	TH:	(none)
Table body	TB:	(none)
Table row	TR:	(none)
Table cell	TC:	(none)
System variable	SV:	Variable format name
User variable	UV:	Variable format name
Graphic (anchored frame or imported object)	G:	(none)
Footnote	F:	Location of footnote: Table or Flow
Marker	M:	Marker type
Cross-reference	X:	Cross-reference format
Text Inset	TI:	(none)
Equation	Q:	Size of equation: Small, Medium, or Large
Element	E:	Element tag (used to wrap elements in higher-level elements)

In Column 2:

- Type the object identifier **E:** (optional)
- Followed by an element tag

In Column 3, type a qualifier (optional) for the new element tag

Qualifier is used in later rules to differentiate elements of the same name when wrapping in higher-level elements

If wrapping a sequence of elements, in Column 1:

- Type **E:** for element
- Type an element tag
- Type a qualifier (optional) in brackets
- Add more element tags with code identifiers
- Use symbols to further describe the sequence

Symbol	Meaning
Plus sign (+)	Item is required and can occur more than once
Question mark (?)	Item is optional and can occur once
Asterisk (*)	Item is optional and can occur more than once
Comma (,)	Items must occur in the order given
Ampersand (&)	Items can occur in any order
Vertical bar (|)	Any one of the items in the sequence can occur
Parentheses	Beginning and end of a sequence

To add an Attribute for Element, in Column 2:

- Type the attribute name and value in brackets after the element tag in the second column of the table
- Separate the name and value with an equal sign, and enclose the value in double quotation marks

If naming a table element from one or more child elements, in Column 1:

- Type the object identifier **TE:**
- Followed by **E:**
- Followed by an element tag
- Type a qualifier (optional) in brackets

To promote anchored objects, in Column 2:

- Type the element tag for the table or graphic
- Add the keyword "**promote**" in parentheses after the element tag for the table or graphic

To flag format overrides, in Column 1:

- Add the rule "**flag paragraph format overrides**"
- Add the rule "**flag character format overrides**"

To wrap untagged text:

- In Column 1, add the rule "**untagged character formatting**"
- In Column 2, add an element tag

Exercise 2: Writing Rules for Text Ranges

In this exercise, you will modify the existing rules for text ranges to match the element tags in **Final EDD.fm.**

1. Locate the following rule:

Wrap this object or objects	In this element	With this qualifier
C:Emphasis	Emphasis	

2. Rewrite the rule as follows:

C:Emphasis	WarnNote	

Text using character tag **Emphasis** should be wrapped in **WarnNote**. Once wrapped, the **Emphasis** character tag is not necessary, as the **TextFormatRules** for **WarnNote** specify the formatting of **Angle Italic.**

3. Find and delete the following rule entirely:

Wrap this object or objects	In this element	With this qualifier
C:WarnNote	WarnNote	

Text using character tag **WarnNote** does not need to be wrapped. This text corresponds with the prefix for the **WarnNote** element. This rule is not necessary at all, as the **PrefixRules** for **WarnNote** specify the formatting of **Color Red.**

4. Save your changes.

Exercise 3: Writing Rules for Paragraphs

In this exercise, you will modify the existing rules for paragraphs to match the element tags in **Final EDD.fm.**

1. Locate the following rules:

Wrap this object or objects	In this element	With this qualifier
P:H1	H1	
P:H2	H2	
P:H3	H3	

2. Rewrite as follows:

P:H1	Head	SH1
P:H2	Head	SH2
P:H3	Head	SH3

- Text using paragraph tag **H1** should be wrapped in **Head**. To differentiate this **Head** from **Head** elements at other nesting levels, give it a qualifier of **SH1**.
- Text using paragraph tag **H2** should be wrapped in **Head**. To differentiate this **Head** from other **Head** elements, give it a qualifier of **SH2**.
- Text using paragraph tag **H3** should be wrapped in **Head**. To differentiate this **Head** from other **Head** elements, give it a qualifier of **SH3**.

3. Locate the following rules:

Wrap this object or objects	In this element	With this qualifier
P:Regular	Regular	
P:Bulleted	Bulleted	
P:Indented	Indented	
P:StepFirst	StepFirst	
P:Step	Step	

4. Rewrite the following rules:

P:Regular	Para	Regular
P:Bulleted	Para	Bull
P:Indented	Para	Substep
P:StepFirst	Para	Step1
P:Step	Para	Step

- Text using paragraph tag **Regular** should be wrapped in **Para**. To differentiate this **Para** from **Para** elements within lists, give it a qualifier of **Regular**.
- Text using paragraph tag **Bulleted** should be wrapped in **Para**. To differentiate this **Para** which appears within a bulleted list, give it a qualifier of **Bull**.
- Text using paragraph tag **Indented** should be wrapped in **Para**. To differentiate this **Para** which serves as a substep to bulleted or numbered items in **List** elements, give it a qualifier of **Substep**.
- Text using paragraph tag **StepRestart** should be wrapped in **Para**. To differentiate this **Para** which restarts a numbered list, give it a qualifier of **Step1**.
- Text using paragraph tag **Step** should be wrapped in **Para**. To differentiate this **Para** which continues a numbered list, give it a qualifier of **Step**.

5. Find the following rule:

Wrap this object or objects	In this element	With this qualifier
P:Note	Note	

6. Rewrite the rule as follows:

P:Note	WarnNote	

Text using paragraph tag **Note** should be wrapped in **WarnNote**.

7. Save your changes.

Exercise 4:   Writing Rules for Footnotes

In this exercise, you will modify the existing rules for footnotes to match the element tags in `Conversion Table.fm`.

1. Locate the following rule:

Wrap this object or objects	In this element	With this qualifier
F:flow	FOOTNOTE	

2. Rewrite the following rule:

F:flow	Footnote	

Footnotes in the main flow should be wrapped in **Footnote** (initial capital letter only).

3. Add the following rule:

F:table	Footnote	

Although you did not have table footnotes in this particular example, you may in other unstructured documents for which you want to use the same conversion table.

4. Save your changes.

Exercise 5:   Writing Rules for Cross-References

In this exercise, you will modify the existing rules for cross-references to match the element tags in **Final EDD.fm**.

1. Locate the following rule:

Wrap this object or objects	In this element	With this qualifier
X:ElemNumTextPage	ElemNumTextPage	

2. Rewrite the following rule:

X:ElemNumTextPage	XRef	

   Cross-references need to be wrapped in **XRef**.

3. Save your changes.

Exercise 6:   Writing Rules for Equations

In this exercise, you will create a rule for equations to match the element tags in **Final EDD.fm**.

1. Add the following rule anywhere in the table:

Wrap this object or objects	In this element	With this qualifier
Q:	EQ (promote)	

   You could specify an equation size of **Small**, **Medium** or **Large**, but you want to wrap all equations in **EQ**, regardless of their size. Adding the word "**(promote)**" makes **EQ** elements a sibling, rather than a child, of the paragraph element in which they are anchored.

2. Save your changes.

Exercise 7:   Writing Rules for Graphics

In this exercise, you will modify the existing rule for graphics to match the element tags in **Final EDD.fm**.

1. Locate the following rule:

Wrap this object or objects	In this element	With this qualifier
G:	GRAPHIC	

2. Rewrite the following rule:

G:	Graphic (promote)	

   Graphics should be wrapped in Graphic (initial capital letter only). Adding the word "**(promote)**" makes them a sibling, rather than a child, of the paragraph element in which they are anchored. According to the EDD, they should be a sibling of **Caption**, not a child.

3. Save your changes.

Exercise 8: Writing Rules for Markers

In this exercise, you will modify the existing rule for index markers and delete the rule for cross-reference markers to match the element tags in **Final EDD.fm**.

1. Locate the following rules:

Wrap this object or objects	In this element	With this qualifier
M:Index	Index	
M:Cross-Ref	Cross-Ref	

2. Rewrite the following rule:

M:Index	IndexEntry	

   Index markers should be wrapped in IndexEntry.

3. Delete the second rule entirely.

   Cross-Ref markers should not be wrapped. You will be using element-based cross-referencing based on attributes.

4. Save your changes.

Exercise 9: Writing Rules for Tables and Table Parts

In this exercise, you will modify the existing rules for tables and table parts to match the element tags in **Final EDD.fm**.

1. Locate the following rules:

Wrap this object or objects	In this element	With this qualifier
P:TableTitle	TableTitle	
P:Pname	Pname	
P:Pnum	Pnum	
P:Pcount	Pcount	
T:Format A	FormatA	

2. Delete the following rules.

P:TableTitle	TableTitle	
P:Pname	Pname	
P:Pnum	Pnum	
P:Pcount	Pcount	

Because you are not allowing elements within the TableTitle, just <TEXT>, you do not need a rule for wrapping the P:TableTitle in an element.

Because you are not allowing elements within the cells of the table, just <TEXT>, you do not need a rule for wrapping the cells' paragraphs in elements before wrapping them in table cell elements.

3. Rewrite the following rule for the table element.

T:Format A	PartsTable (promote)

Table elements should use PartsTable. Adding the word "(promote)" makes them a sibling, rather than a child, of the paragraph element in which they are anchored.

4. Locate the following rules:

Wrap this object or objects	In this element	With this qualifier
TT:	TITLE	
TH:	HEADING	
TB:	BODY	
TF:	FOOTING	
TR:	ROW	
TC:	CELL	

5. Rewrite the following rules for the table heading, table body, and table footing elements.

TH:	TableHeading
TB:	TableBody
TF:	TableFooting

These are the elements defined in your EDD.

6. Rewrite the following rule for the table row element.

TR:	PartRow

This is the element name defined in your EDD.

7. Rewrite the following rule for the table cell element.

TC:P:Pname	PartName

The paragraph (using Pname format) in the cell will be wrapped directly in the table cell element with the tag PartName.

8. Add the following two rules:

TC:P:Pnum	PartNum
TC:P:Pcount	PartCount

The paragraph (using Pnum format) in the cell will be wrapped directly in the table cell element with the element tag PartNum. Pcount will be wrapped in PartCount.

9. Save your changes.

Exercise 10: Wrapping Captions and Graphics in Figures

In this exercise, you will add a rule to group the Caption and Graphic together in a Figure element.

1. Add the following rule:

Wrap this object or objects	In this element	With this qualifier
E:Caption?, E:Graphic	Figure	

Although your EDD requires the Caption, you will make it optional in the wrapping process. In case an author forgot the Caption, Graphic will still be wrapped in Figure, with a square hole displaying in the **Structure View** where the Caption is missing.

Your goal is to wrap as much as possible, even if the unstructured document does not quite conform to the element definitions defined in the EDD. In the end, you will have less manual wrapping to do.

2. Save your changes.

Exercise 11: Wrapping Paras in Items in Lists

In this exercise, you will add several rules to wrap the various **Para** elements (by qualifier) in **Item**. Then, you will wrap the **Item** in a **List**.

1. Add the following three rules:

Wrap this object or objects	In this element	With this qualifier
E:Para[Step1], (E:Para[Substep] | E:WarnNote | E:Figure)*	Item	First
E:Para[Step], (E:Para[Substep] | E:WarnNote | E:Figure)*	Item	Additional
E:Para[Bull], (E:Para[Substep] | E:WarnNote | E:Figure)*	Item	BullItem

- First rule wraps a **Para** with qualifier **Step1**—followed by zero or more of **Para** with qualifier **Substep**, **WarnNote**, and **Figure** elements—in an **Item** with qualifier **First**.
- Second rule wraps a **Para** with qualifier **Step**—followed by zero or more of **Para** with qualifier **Substep**, **WarnNote**, and **Figure** elements—in an **Item** with qualifier **Additional**.
- Third rule wraps a **Para** with qualifier **Bull**—followed by zero or more of **Para** with qualifier **Substep**, **WarnNote**, and **Figure** elements—in an **Item** with qualifier **BullItem** (watch the spelling).

2. Add the following two rules:

Wrap this object or objects	In this element	With this qualifier
E:Item[BullItem]+	List [ListType = "Bulleted"]	
E:Item[First], E:Item[Additional]*	List [ListType = "Numbered"]	

- First rule wraps one or more **Item** elements with qualifier **BullItem** in a **List** with the **ListType** attribute and a value of **Bulleted**, which drives the formatting of bulleted lists in your EDD.

- Second rule wraps one **Item** element with qualifier **First**—followed by zero or more **Item** elements with qualifier **Additional**—in a **List** with the **ListType** attribute and a value of **Numbered**, which drives the formatting of numbered lists in your EDD.

- Again, to maximize the amount of automatic wrapping, the conversion rules for the number of items in a list can be less restrictive than the actual rules in the EDD. (EDD requires two, conversion rules require only one.) Missing required elements will display as square holes in the **Structure View**.

3. Save your changes.

Exercise 12: **Wrapping Heads and Their Siblings in Sections**

In this exercise, you will add several rules to wrap the various **Head** elements (by qualifier) and their siblings in a **Section**.

1. Add the following three rules:

Wrap this object or objects	In this element	With this qualifier
E:Head[SH3], (E:Para[Regular] | E:List | E:PartsTable | E:Figure | E:EQ | E:WarnNote)+	Section	Section3
E:Head[SH2], (E:Para[Regular] | E:List | E:PartsTable | E:Figure | E:EQ | E:WarnNote | Section[Section3])+	Section	Section2
E:Head[SH1], (E:Para[Regular] | E:List | E:PartsTable | E:Figure | E:EQ | E:WarnNote | Section[Section2])+	Section	Section1

- First rule wraps a 3rd-level **Head** and its siblings in a **Section** with qualifier **Section3**.

- Second rule wraps a 2nd-level **Head** and its siblings (some of which can be a 3rd-level **Section**) in a **Section** with qualifier **Section2**.

- Third rule wraps a 1st-level **Head** and its siblings (some of which can be a 2nd-level **Section**) in a **Section** with qualifier **Section1**.

- Again, to maximize the amount of automatic wrapping, the conversion rules for the number of a subordinate-level **Section** within a parent **Section** are less restrictive than those in the EDD.

2. Save your changes.

Exercise 13: Wrapping the Highest-Level Element

In this exercise, you will add one rule to wrap up the entire document.

1. Add the following rule:

E:Title, E:Section[Section1]+	Chapter

Again, to maximize the amount of automatic wrapping, the conversion rule doesn't require more than one **Section** in the **Chapter**. As long as you import element definitions from a structured template or EDD in the document you are wrapping, missing and misplaced elements will be found when validating.

2. Save your changes.

Completed Conversion Table

Wrap this object or objects	In this element	With this qualifier
P:Title	Title	
P:H1	Head	SH1
P:H2	Head	SH2
P:H3	Head	SH3
P:Regular	Para	Regular
P:Bulleted	Para	Bull
P:Caption	Caption	
P:Indented	Para	Substep
P:StepFirst	Para	Step1
P:Step	Para	Step
P:Note	WarnNote	
C:Emphasis	WarnNote	
X:ElemNumTextPage	XRef	
M:Index	IndexEntry	
Q:	EQ	
G:	Graphic (promote)	
F:flow	Footnote	
F:table	Footnote	

Wrap this object or objects	In this element	With this qualifier
T:Format A	PartsTable (promote)	
TT:	TableTitle	
TH:	TableHeading	
TB:	TableBody	
TF:	TableFooting	
TR:	PartRow	
TC:P:Pname	PartName	
TC:P:Pnum	PartNum	
TC:P:Pcount	PartCount	
E:Caption, E:Graphic	Figure	
E:Para[Step1], (E:Para[Substep] | E:WarnNote | E:Figure)*	Item	First
E:Para[Step], (E:Para[Substep] | E:WarnNote | E:Figure)*	Item	Additional
E:Para[Bull], (E:Para[Substep] | E:WarnNote | E:Figure)*	Item	BullItem
E:Item[BullItem]+	List [ListType = "Bulleted"]	
E:Item[First], E:Item[Additional]*	List [ListType = "Numbered"]	
E:Head[SH3], (E:Para[Regular] | E:List | E:PartsTable | E:Figure | E:EQ | E:WarnNote)+	Section	Section3
E:Head[SH2], (E:Para[Regular] | E:List | E:PartsTable | E:Figure | E:EQ | E:WarnNote | Section[Section3])+	Section	Section2
E:Head[SH1], (E:Para[Regular] | E:List | E:PartsTable | E:Figure | E:EQ | E:WarnNote | Section[Section2])+	Section	Section1
E:Title, E:Section[Section1]+	Chapter	

Structuring Unstructured Documents

You can structure:

- Single files
- Groups of files
- Books and their component files

 Exercise 14: Structuring Current Unstructured Document

In this exercise, you will structure a single file using your conversion table.

1. If not still open, from your class files directory, open **Conversion Table.fm**.

   If you did not finish the conversion table, please open **Final Conversion Table.fm Conversion Table.fm** instead, and save it in your class files directory as **Conversion Table.fm**.

 If you have difficulty with the table you created, the **Final Conversion Table.fm** document can help you troubleshoot your conversion rules to find typos or mistakes.

2. From your class files directory, open **Final EDD.fm**.

3. If not still open, from your class files directory, open **wraptest.fm**.

4. In **wraptest.fm**, import element definitions from **Final EDD.fm**

   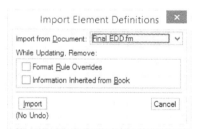

   a. From the **File** menu in `wraptest.fm`, choose **Import > Element Definitions**.

   b. From the **Import from Document** popup menu, choose **Final EDD.fm**.

   c. Click **Import**.

      An alert box appears indicating "**Element definitions have been imported from the EDD**"

   d. Click **OK** to close any alerts.

5. Save your changes.

6. From the **File** menu in **wraptest.fm**, choose **Utilities > Structure Current Document**.

   The **Structure Current Document** dialog appears

7. From the **Conversion Table Document** popup menu, choose **Conversion Table.fm**.

8. Click **Add Structure**.

   Alert appears indicating "**Operation completed normally.**"

9. Click **OK** to dismiss the alert.

   If there were errors, a log file appears diagnosing the errors.

10. If necessary, modify **Conversion Table.fm** and repeat the conversion.

    A new **NoName** document appears with the initial file's contents wrapped according to the rules in the conversion table.

11. Save the file as `wraptest.out.fm`.

12. Validate and correct any validation errors.

    You will need to correct a missing attribute value for the **Author** attribute and fix some unresolved cross-references, relinking them to **PartsTable** and **Figure** elements, rather than paragraphs.

13. If elements do not appear to be wrapped correctly, modify **Conversion Table.fm** and restructure the **wraptest.fm** file, not the output file which is already wrapped.

14. Save and close all your files.

Need FrameMaker Training?

Train with Tech Comm Tools

High Value

Each course has all of the content from my 100% live classes, along with an ever-growing library of in-depth material I've created in response to individual student needs.

Easy to access

Each week you'll have live reviews, recorded lessons for key features, and relevant exercises. Can't make a live session? They're all recorded, so you review at your convenience.

In-Depth

Honestly, you wouldn't want this much content in a 2-day class! But topics are marked as either CORE or TARGETED to let you get what you need without spending time on features that don't apply to your work.

Visit bit.ly/tc2ls-courses to see course schedule and syllabi

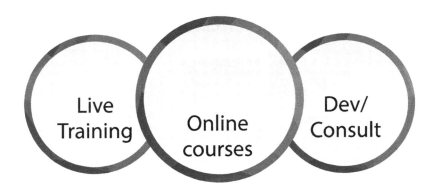

CPSIA information can be obtained
at www.ICGtesting.com
Printed in the USA
LVHW100737090620
657582LV00012B/565